REVOKING CITIZENSHIP

Revoking Citizenship

Expatriation in America from the Colonial Era to the War on Terror

Ben Herzog

With a foreword by Ediberto Román

NEW YORK UNIVERSITY PRESS

New York and London

NEW YORK UNIVERSITY PRESS
New York and London
www.nyupress.org

First published in paperback in 2017

References to Internet websites (URLs) were accurate at the time of writing. Neither the author nor New York University Press is responsible for URLs that may have expired or changed since the manuscript was prepared.

Library of Congress Cataloging-in-Publication Data
Herzog, Ben, author.
Revoking citizenship : expatriation in America from the Colonial era to the War on Terror / Ben Herzog ; with a foreword by Ediberto Román.
pages cm — (Citizenship and migration in the Americas)
Includes bibliographical references and index.
ISBN 978-0-8147-6038-3 (cl : alk. paper)
ISBN 978-1-4798-7771-3 (pb : alk. paper)
1. Expatriation — United States--History. 2. Citizenship — United States — History.
3. United States — Emigration and immigration — Government policy.
4. Nationalism — United States. I. Title. II. Title: Expatriation in America from the Colonial era to the War on Terror III. Series: Citizenship and migration in the Americas.
KF4715.H47   2015
323.6'40973--dc23   2014040535

New York University Press books are printed on acid-free paper, and their binding materials are chosen for strength and durability. We strive to use environmentally responsible suppliers and materials to the greatest extent possible in publishing our books.

Manufactured in the United States of America

10 9 8 7 6 5 4 3 2 1

Also available as an ebook

To my beautiful girls,
Taly, Ofer, Tomer, and Dana

CONTENTS

TABLES AND FIGURES

Figures

Tables

FOREWORD

EDIBERTO ROMÁN

Citizenship, considered the most basic of all rights, is also known as the right to have rights. Despite what appears to be its central and foundational nature, the concept is under fire. Such a state of affairs seems odd, as one would naturally think that a concept so fundamental and so closely associated with democratic order would not be the subject of debate. Indeed, it is a term that dates back to the Greco-Roman era, when giants like Aristotle extolled its virtues as well as its importance to democratic forms of government. It is a concept with countless examples of struggles for its attainment throughout the annals of time, with peoples fighting to acquire this all-important status, and even more to preserve it. Indeed, the very thought of citizenship evokes an association with equality as well as the belief in the superiority of democracies over other forms of government. Unquestionably, historical examples of efforts to obtain and retain rights of citizenship are both vivid and sobering, from the struggle for women's rights in the United States, which lasted over a century, to the current struggle for domestic civil rights and marriage equality. People live and fight for the status that citizenship is supposed to provide.

One would therefore expect that this hallowed concept is fully understood, respected, and equally viewed as immutable. One might think all these things, but nothing could be farther from the truth. There is no legal, political, and cultural concept that is currently more contested. With increased racial, ethnic, and other forms of diversity in our society, more and more calls have recently been made to limit, change, or do away with our traditional view of citizenship, as well as the means to attain it.

In the United States, perhaps the most glaring and controversial attacks on the concept arose not long after the election of the first

African American president, Barak Obama. The self-described Birthers repeatedly asserted, despite ample evidence to the contrary, that President Obama is ineligible for high office because he is not a natural-born citizen; they claimed instead that he was actually born in Kenya. Despite a wealth of evidence to the contrary, including an actual certificate of live birth from the state of Hawaii, these challenges have persisted well into Obama's second term in office, leading many to believe they are a pretext for racial animus. According to the Birthers, the fact that President Obama has an East African Islamic name indicates that he is really not "American." For these self-proclaimed patriots, his not having an Anglo-Saxon Christian name means that he must be an outsider. And since his father was from Kenya, President Obama cannot be a legitimate president. In effect, the Birthers seem to be adding another prerequisite for citizenship, one that goes beyond proof of birthright citizenship.

Another forceful domestic attack on citizenship has occurred in the arena of the country's ongoing immigration debate. In what many view as merely another pretext to push forward racist policy, the Birthers have been attempting to repeal birthright citizenship. Their claim, with virtually no evidentiary or empirical support, is that pregnant undocumented immigrants cross the border and have their children in the United States in order to take advantage of birthright citizenship. These so-called "anchor babies," according to the Birthers, eventually enable entire undocumented families to obtain U.S. citizenship. Though this second claim is bereft of any factual support, and fails to even recognize that natural born immigrant children cannot petition for their immediate family members, which is a cumbersome process in and of itself, until they reach adulthood, it has captured considerable public attention.

These attacks on citizenship on the part of the Birthers have led to a slow but growing movement to repeal portions of the Fourteenth Amendment to the Constitution, which specifically grants citizenship to those born in the United States, either directly or indirectly. For instance, rather than attempting to alter the Constitution, a bill introduced by Congressman Steve King seeks to amend the Immigration and Nationality Act to "require that only the children of citizens . . . be granted citizenship." This bill picked up over a dozen cosponsors the first day it was introduced.

The attacks on citizenship are not limited to the domestic arena, unfortunately. Just a few months ago, the Dominican Republic's high court ruled that all children born of immigrant parents could not claim Dominican citizenship. This conclusion was not just inconsistent with pertinent Dominican constitutional provisions; it flew in the face of a previous Inter-American Court on Human Rights decision on the very same matter. The challenge to citizenship is even more radical, though, in that the court not only did away with classic birthright, or *jus solis*, citizenship, but also, shockingly, applied its decision retroactively for nearly a hundred years. Thus, in this hemisphere's most recent attack on citizenship, the citizenship of hundreds of thousands of nationals was stripped away overnight under what the Dominican government is now asserting was an immigration control measure. This obfuscating and absurd justification utterly fails to appreciate that citizens are not historically treated as foreigners or immigrants. Or are they?

In *Revoking Citizenship: Expatriation in America from the Colonial Era to the War on Terror*, Professor Ben Herzog brings to light one of the most telling and troubling recent developments in citizenship debates and policies—the taking away of this cherished status. In an exhaustive and enlightening analysis of the ease with which we as a country appear to be ready to revoke citizenship under the guise of national security, Herzog starts by examining recent efforts to strip a U.S. citizen of his status despite both the wishes of the citizen and the absence of any criminal conviction against him. From this troubling and true account of Yasser Hamdi, Herzog goes on to write a fascinating and provocative history of the revocation of citizenship, one that goes beyond traditional legal discussions and explores the cultural and political dimensions of governmental efforts to take away the most basic of all rights. Indeed, what Herzog produces is an exhaustive examination of U.S. efforts to make citizens "stateless," a status that is recognized as one of the most dreadful political fates that can befall anyone in the modern world.

In so doing, Herzog provides much needed contextualization for what many incorrectly believe is a new phenomenon. His is the hitherto little-known account of a practice that has been part of American policy since the end of the nineteenth century. Equally important, this work addresses an area that scholars have largely avoided. While most recent works on the citizenship focus on the entrance of immigrants into the national community and focus on an understanding of "who" should belong to the national "we," as historian Eric Foner recently addressed in his work on *Who Owns History*. Herzog's critical work examines the converse, focusing on "who" are those that should be removed from the collective "us."

In the end, Herzog posits that expatriation policy is an attempt to regulate and enforce the national world order, and places the revocation of citizenship within this sociological framework. Perhaps one of the most important contributions of this project is that it will change the focus of citizenship debates from inclusionary to exclusionary practices. In doing so, this book is sure to promote strong reactions and responses, as well as to stimulate further discussion of one of the more challenging constitutional issues of our day. Indeed, *Revoking Citizenship* will surely be the leading work on the subject for decades to come.

ACKNOWLEDGMENTS

I am grateful to all who offered assistance, encouragement, and advice on this book. In particular, I owe a special debt of gratitude to Ivan Szelenyi and Julia Adams, who have been both mentors and friends. I also wish to thank Philip Gorski, Adriana Kemp, Nadim Rouhana, Gil Eyal, Chad Alan Goldberg, Jack Goldstone, Ilan Peleg, Pnina Lahav, Linda Kerber, and Gerhard Casper for their suggestions and comments. Support from New York University Press and its editors has been most valuable, and special thanks go to Deborah Gershenowitz and Ediberto Román, who did not stop believing in my work. Completing this book would not have been possible without the generous help of my friends, family, librarians, anonymous reviewers, conference commentators, and workshop attendees, as well institutional support from the Jackson Institute for Global Affairs at Yale University and the Canada Program at the Weatherhead Center for International Affairs at Harvard University. Last but not least, I would not be writing this acknowledgment were it not for my endless love for Taly, Ofer, Tomer, and Dana.

Introduction

> To be a stateless individual is one of the most dreadful
> political fates that can befall anyone in the modern world.
> And the possession of an American passport particularly is
> profoundly valued, especially by naturalized citizens.
> —Judith N. Shklar, *American Citizenship:*
> *The Quest for Inclusion*

In late November 2001, after the United States' invasion of Afghanistan, hundreds of surrendering Taliban fighters were sent to the Qala-e-Jangi prison complex near Mazari Sharif. Among the surrendering Taliban forces were Afghan Arabs who instigated a prison riot by detonating grenades they had concealed in their clothing, attacking Northern Alliance guards, and seizing weapons. The prison uprising was brought to an end after a three-day battle that included heavy air support from U.S. AC-130 gunships and Black Hawk helicopters. One American soldier was killed and nine were injured along with about fifty Northern Alliance soldiers. Between 200 and 400 Taliban prisoners were killed during the prison uprising. Among the Taliban survivors were Yaser Esam Hamdi and John Walker Lindh, who were also American citizens.

Hamdi was named in the media as the "accidental citizen" or the "second American Taliban." The Bush administration described him as an "illegal enemy combatant" and detained him for almost three years without charging him with any crime. He was initially detained at Camp X-Ray at the U.S. naval base in Guantanamo Bay, Cuba, and was later transferred to military jails in Virginia and South Carolina after it became known that he was a U.S. citizen.

In June 2004, the United States Supreme Court rejected the U.S. government's attempts to detain Hamdi indefinitely without trial. On September 23, 2004, the United States Justice Department released Hamdi to Saudi Arabia without charge on the condition that he renounce his U.S. citizenship.

This case has many legal aspects for study. Among them are the separation of powers among the branches of the government, the detention of noncombatant Americans, and the legality of Hamdi's "voluntary" renunciation of citizenship. Throughout this book, I locate the sociological and symbolic meanings of taking away citizenship as in the case presented above. Why do states take away citizenship from their subjects? When do states expatriate their citizens and with what justification? Should loyalty be judged according to birthplace or actions? Should it be judged at all? Above all, I ask whether citizenship and the rights associated with it can be multiple or divided. The policies of revoking citizenship will be the lens through which I examine, describe, and analyze the complex relationships among citizenship, immigration, the national logic, and ideology.

Stripping away citizenship and all the rights that come with it is usually associated with despotic and totalitarian regimes. The imagery of mass expulsion of once-integral members of the community is associated with such events as civil war, ethnic cleansing, the Holocaust, or other oppressive historical events. It is not surprising to hear that this practice was used in the past by South Africa's apartheid regime, by Germany during both world wars, by Stalinist Russia, pre-1789 France, and the Roman Empire.[1] Although related, these practices are not just a product of undemocratic events or extreme situations, but are standard clauses within the legal systems of most democratic states, including the United States. Here, both naturalized immigrants and native-born American citizens have been judged to be un-American and had their citizenship stripped away.

The recent, and continuing, "War on Terror" has made civil rights a core topic of discussion. We have been witness to the fact that citizenship, once taken for granted as inalienable, can be revoked even from native-born Americans. But the real news is that this practice has been part of American policy since the end of the nineteenth century. *Revoking Citizenship* sheds light on the current state of this practice by looking at its transformation throughout the years and across countries. Thus, the study of the revocation of citizenship simultaneously informs us about topical events (such as the Hamdi case, Patriot Act II, or Lieberman's terrorist expatriation act) and provides us with insight into the nature of rights in the modern world in general.

The common thread in most of the recent studies on citizenship is that immigration and naturalization processes are articulated in relation to the conception of citizenship and nationhood in any particular country.[2] That is, the regulations responsible for the entrance into and inclusion of new members in the national community are dependent on the understanding of who should belong to the national "we" and who should not. In this research study, I examine the converse of these laws—those measures that deal with legally excluding people from membership in the political community or loss of citizenship.

Of course, the formal revocation of citizenship is not the only way to curtail American citizenship. An even more widespread phenomenon is the revocation of certain citizenship rights from an American citizen. On September 30, 2011, Anwar al-Awlaki, a radical American-born Muslim cleric who became a leading figure in Al Qaeda, was killed in Yemen by a missile fired from an American drone aircraft. Assassination of an American citizen without trial might be an extreme example, but millions of Americans lose some of their citizenship rights every day. Measures include, but are not limited to, depriving convicted felons of voting rights; denial of full citizenship for children; in the past, unequal citizenship rights for women and nonwhites; racial barriers to immigration or the curtailment of some social rights—such as minimum wage or the right to unionize—for workfare workers.[3] In this book, I limit the discussion of exclusion to the formal and total revocation of citizenship.

The analytical move of shifting the focus of the academic study of citizenship from inclusionary to exclusionary practices is more than an empirical innovation. From a theoretical perspective, scholars of citizenship have traditionally discussed two issues. On the one hand, many have asked who is allowed to join each state and become a full citizen. While the study of the recruitment of new members to the nation-state stands at the foundation of cutting-edge research on citizenship, the investigation of the notion of annulment or revocation of citizenship is usually ignored. On the other hand, scholars have questioned what rights and responsibilities are associated with the legal status of citizenship. I suggest that there is another element of citizenship that we should study. That is, we should investigate the meaning of the tie between the individual and the state, the social and cultural assumptions behind it, and the social order that citizenship represents. Can citizenship be transferred, removed, divided, or be multiple?

The myth of a tight fit between the perceived ethnic, religious, cultural, or political borders of nationality and the territorial borders of the nation-state has always been challenged by population movement and conflicting citizenship laws. Expatriation can be seen as an attempt to regulate and enforce the national world order. In this book I use the concept of "national world order" to describe the hegemonic geopolitical perception that the world is divided to distinct national entities. The practice of taking away citizenship was mainly introduced to eliminate dual citizenship, which poses great difficulty for the national logic. That is, regardless of the particular type of citizenship, multiple allegiances threaten the comprehensiveness of the national ideal. In order to trace the emergence of this practice, I will follow the discussions of it in the United States.

Until the second half of the twentieth century, the United States shared with other countries the national ideal that accepted the transfer of national allegiance, and indeed its birth involved asserting the necessity of that transfer, but a suspicion of divided national loyalty persisted. Thus, the United States enacted grounds for expatriation in order to regulate the exclusivity of nationality. The U.S. case is significant as this practice goes side by side with (and sometimes in opposition to) one of the core American political values—the idea that citizenship should be voluntary and contractual. This book shows that this political idea can turn in some circumstances from making the individual safer to threatening him or her, when the contract is questioned by the state. I argue that the practice of expatriation is contingent on particular political or practical circumstances (such as military conflicts, immigration needs, consular dilemmas, and changing international norms).[4] However, expatriation has usually been initiated in order to regulate the national world order and the national logic that accompanied it.

U.S. laws, international treaties, consular correspondences, and legislative debates regarding states' rights to revoke citizenship and citizens' privileges to renounce the same citizenship show that these rights are dependent on the national logic. As stated previously, it is the same national logic that prohibits dual or multiple citizenship.

Whether citizenship is understood as a coherent worldview, or whether it is seen as a more-or-less integrated bundle of variegated practices and policies (typically generated in different periods and under distinctive circumstances), the concept of citizenship is tied to the national logic.

The United States may be the best case study of the policy of revocation of citizenship. In contrast to totalitarian regimes that tend to denationalize their opposition and have few legal barriers against this action, I expected that the constitutional-democratic political institutions in the United States would have positioned it as the least likely state to strip away citizenship.[5] Hence, by studying the revocation of citizenship in the American context, I can clarify and test accepted hypotheses and generate new theoretical propositions regarding the relation between citizens and the state.

In the United States, taking away citizenship has been justified on the grounds that the citizen has transferred his or her national allegiance. Changing citizenship has been central to American political philosophy from the American Revolution (when settlers were to be allowed to make the break with England) until today. Individual behavior and attitudes (in contrast to ascriptive belonging) were much more likely to appeal to Americans as a valid reason for taking away citizenship. Thus, although expatriation policies appeared in the United States only at the end of the nineteenth century, the investigation of this concept should start earlier, with the unique conception of the linkage between the individual and state formulated by the American colonists.

Looking at expatriation laws, I argue that the policy of taking away citizenship is an attempt to regulate and enforce the national world order. The practice of taking away citizenship was introduced largely to eliminate dual citizenship, which poses a great challenge to the national logic that assumes full loyalty to one's nation-state. Throughout the book, we will look at the initiation of expatriation policies in the United States. Indeed, I found that the United States was suspicious of divided national loyalty and established grounds for expatriation in order to regulate the singularity of nationality. However, we will also see that since the 1950s, the United States began, *de jure* and sometimes *de facto*, to reduce the usage of this practice. This book explains this process as well.

I show that the United States did not restrict its expatriation policies because it suddenly accepted multiple national allegiances. Accommodating dual citizenship, which is tolerated in the United States, is not directly related to a specific ideology but is a practical response to changing domestic and international laws; to national stresses such as rebellion, immigration, or military conflicts; or to the impossibility of regulating exclusive national allegiance in the globalized world. The first two historical phases of citizenship (non-changeable and single citizenship) can be traced to two complementary philosophical stages (biological and contractual citizenship) and are related to institutional changes (from monarchies to republics). However, accepting dual citizenship fits only a speculative philosophy that imagines a cosmopolitan world.

In the first chapter, I introduce the theoretical foundations of the study of citizenship and its revocation. Why is citizenship fundamental for possessing rights? What happens when citizenship is taken away, and what are the differences and similarities between the various conceptions of modern citizenship? In this addressing these questions, I place the revocation of citizenship into a sociological framework as well as comparative-historical context.[6]

What is the difference between citizenship and pre-modern political memberships? In the second chapter, I present the philosophical ideals and the practical considerations that brought Americans to construct a different conception of citizenship from that of the British "motherland." This individualistic new citizenship regime allows and even encourages the transfer of citizenship in some instances. Individual autonomy is one of the pillars of legal attempts in the United States to hold the individual responsible to the national order.[7] However, I argue that while those concerns brought about the right of renunciation, they did not change the national ideal of exclusive citizenship.

The third chapter is devoted to the initiation of expatriation laws in the United States. Since the Civil War, the United States' policy has fluctuated between different (and sometimes opposing) principles and forms of expatriation. This book seeks to unify and find pattern in history, as well as recognizing a diversity of causal factors. Although the American political philosophy that led to the separation of the American colonies from Britain accepted the transfer of national allegiance, representatives of the American state were suspicious of divided national loyalties. In presenting the reader with the complete list of bills introduced regarding the loss of citizenship, I argue that the United States enacted grounds for expatriation in order to regulate the exclusivity of American nationality.

The policy of expatriation was influenced and sometimes dictated by international relations between the United States and both its allies and its enemies. The fourth chapter follows those considerations by looking at the treaties the United States signed regarding expatriation. I found that while some of the expatriation policies were constructed in response to the ideology of exclusive national allegiance, others were overturned as practical responses to the state's immediate needs in the international arena (mainly in respect to military efforts). Protecting the national order is vulnerable to other, nonmilitary exigencies, and this accounts for much of the complexity of the history of the legislation and the conversation around it.

In the fifth chapter, I present the initial practical dilemmas that led the Department of State to adopt the policy of exclusive nationality. Letters and circulars exchanged between Washington and the consulates around the world show the need for a concrete and coherent policy regarding expatriation both before and after the legislation of the expatriation acts in Congress. I show how the actual concerns of diplomatic and consular officers shaped the practice of expatriation. This is not to say that the national world order is ultimately generated from the ground up, but that the details of its regulation in war and peace and different economic and ideological circumstances are how the national world order is regulated and performed. A constant supply of boundary issues does not undermine the order generating them.

The sixth chapter brings to the fore the current American perspective on taking away citizenship. Several decisions of the Supreme Court have shifted the benchmark for stripping away citizenship. In the past, the policy of expatriation was mainly introduced as a punishment for un-American activities. Even though the cases are few and in a sense marginal, high publicity cases can reinforce an ideology of belonging; through them, a message and a warning is sent out about what it means to be a good citizen. Since the late 1950s, special emphasis has been placed on the intent behind expatriation. Citizenship can be revoked only after the state shows there was a voluntary intent to relinquish this status. Chapter 6 thus reveals the conflicting political and philosophical ideals that govern this approach.

Following the Supreme Court rulings and the ensuing legislative changes, the State Department appointed the Board of Appellate Review to oversee the department's expatriation decisions. The goal was to detect whether the Department of State had satisfied the burden of proof that the appellant's expatriation act was performed with the intent to relinquish United States citizenship. In the seventh chapter, I follow the board's decisions since 1980 and show that while the board's deliberations do incorporate the idea of intent, it also continues to uphold the principle that nationality should not be divided. As will be seen, the real-world motives of individuals did not so easily fit into a rigid scheme of voluntary allegiance as defined by bureaucracy and the courts.

In practice, the United States has abandoned the ideal of undivided national membership. Although all current and past administrations officially oppose dual citizenship, millions of Americans have multiple national identities, and the United States tolerate this situation. The eighth chapter discusses recent developments in the policy of expatriation in light of the War on Terror. By looking at several proposals for new expatriation laws, I present the reemergence of the idea of the exclusiveness of national belonging, which applies even to native-born Americans and even when it contradicts the Supreme Court's rulings.

In the ninth chapter, I argue that the practice of taking away citizenship was mainly introduced to eliminate dual citizenship, a status that potentially undermines the national logic that assumes full loyalty to one's nation-state. Indeed, I found that in contrast to the novel American political philosophy that embraced the transfer of national allegiance, the United States continued to be suspicious of divided national loyalty and established grounds for expatriation in order to regulate the singularity of nationality. However, since the middle of the twentieth century, the practice of expatriation has been gradually eliminated. The United States began to tolerate dual citizenship. While the legal ruling on this issue is absolute, the sociological perception that national allegiance ought not to be divided still lingers.

1

Revoking Citizenship

Man, it turns out, can lose all so-called Rights of Man
without losing his essential quality as a man, his human
dignity. Only the loss of a polity itself expels him from
humanity.
—Hannah Arendt, The Origins of Totalitarianism

Why is citizenship fundamental for possessing rights? What happens
when citizenship is taken away? What are the differences and similarities between the different conceptions of modern citizenship? In this
chapter I will try to answer these questions by explaining the theoretical
basis of the study of citizenship and its revocation. I define the concept
of citizenship through exploration of the coherence debate within the
study of citizenship. Then, I explain the notion of the national world system, which I argue is the reason (and justification) for the revocation of
citizenship. The state measure of taking away citizenship has both practical and symbolic significance. I conclude this chapter by explaining
my research design and presenting the policy of taking away American
citizenship and the legal terminology that is utilized to express it. In this
research, I place the revocation of citizenship into a sociological framework as well as a comparative-historical context. The scope of my study
includes not only the actual implemented policy of expatriation, but
also the social and symbolic meanings of such policy. This sociological
framework is illuminated through the analysis of the texts of proposed
and legislated laws; the views of the politicians who introduced those
bills; the reactions of the United States Supreme Court; the interpretations of the State Department; and the positions of international treaties
on this issue.

Defining Citizenship

Citizenship is usually defined (with some variations) as "both a set of practices and a bundle of rights that define an individual's membership in a polity."[1] Yet, defining citizenship as an analytical concept is a presumptuous task for two reasons. First, its definition is highly contested and has competing, if not contradictory, meanings and applications, ranging from the purely legal/bureaucratic to an indicator of status, a form of identity, and a set of practices. Second, this institution is constantly changing and will probably continue to change in the future. Citizenship in its various forms is contingent upon historical struggles and conflicts, and both access to it and the types of privileges and obligations it entails have been contested by various political organizations.

Given the constantly transforming nature of citizenship, I describe it by highlighting one of the important debates regarding the characteristics of citizenship. This debate involves two contradictory views. On one side of the theoretical spectrum are scholars who argue that citizenship is a constant and coherent value that describes both rights and obligations associated with belonging to a particular political entity (usually, a nation-state). The major opposing theory argues that citizenship is neither coherent nor consistent and that the rights and obligations associated with it can have opposing (and sometimes conflicting) rationales, motives, or justifications, even when proposed by the same people. Although scholars have described national citizenship in a variety of additional ways, I claim that all writings on citizenship can be categorized into one of the above-mentioned analytical classifications.

In some instances researchers are aware of this distinction between understanding citizenship as a stable concept and the perception of this status as the outcome of ongoing and everlasting political struggle, and even try to advocate for one perspective over another. For many other scholars of citizenship, this debate is only implied in their writings. Moreover, some of the scholars I mention might even reject my analytical categorization of their own theories. I hope to persuade the reader of the usefulness of this particular classification of theories, at least for the purposes of this book.

According to Brubaker, the difference between Germany and France is in their conception of citizenship. While France's model is one of territorial inclusion and assimilative citizenship (*jus soli*), Germany applies a model of nationhood based on ethnic inclusion (*jus sanguinis*). The former gives priority to the protection of individual rights within the territory of the state, while the latter emphasizes ethnic origin as the criterion for equal citizenship or naturalization. Brubaker invokes a cultural explanation of citizenship, which attributes a *volk*-centered nationhood to Germany and a civic-centered citizenship to France, and argues that these differences arise from particular historical circumstances of state-building. The French nation-state and its national consciousness were gradually developed, and the notion of citizenship was crystallized within the framework of the state during the French Revolution. Conversely, the German national consciousness was for centuries divorced from any cohesive or unified organization (a German state). "The French understand their nation as the creation of their state, the Germans their nation as the basis of their state."[2] While Brubaker's conception of citizenship and nationhood is theoretically contingent on historical circumstances, in reality it is deeply rooted in national self-perception (which is reinforced by its institutionalization in immigration policies) and thus is unlikely to change. Joppke and Roshenhek criticized the shortcomings of the implicit primordialist account in Brubaker's position from 1992 (which he later retracted), especially "the assumption of a 'straight line' between reified and fixed identities and policies, which leaves out the fundamental role of conflict and contingency, that is, politics and history, as intervening variables."[3]

This standpoint, which perceives nationality as a reified and fixed identity, is shared by many people in the academic community and in the general public. The broad generalization of citizenship practices and national culture can be very useful in locating overarching characteristics of large societies. The simplification of the notion of citizenship as consisting of a single and coherent value system is usually a necessity for both comprehending and explaining national trends. Accordingly, many scholars identify a nation-state with a particular coherent citizenship in both descriptive and normative terms.[4] Many others argue that if a single coherent citizenship is not established, a conception of citizenship should be constructed for each specific state.[5]

Brubaker's unitary approach is challenged by Rogers Smith, who claims that the various citizenship principles are neither coherent nor consistent. In other words, at any given time, citizenship is a mix of multiple civic ideas. Smith explores the United States' conception of citizenship by examining all federal statutes and all federal, circuit, and Supreme Court decisions from the nation's origins (1798) to the progressive era (1912), and he argues that three conceptions of citizenship can (and usually do) exist together in the same polity. These three correspond with liberalism, "ascriptive inegalitarianism" (which supports the superiority of the origins of current rulers), and republicanism,[6] which can be expressed simultaneously "in logically inconsistent but politically effective combinations."[7] In his analysis of the American Revolution, de Tocqueville described this nation as an essentially liberal democratic society, especially since it appeared remarkably egalitarian in comparison to the class hierarchies in Europe. Even if some inconsistencies could be pointed out, as in attitudes towards slavery, de Tocqueville depicted them as temporary exceptions likely to dissipate in time, particularly through universal liberal citizenship laws. However, careful analysis of court rulings on important citizenship issues covering three centuries of American history shows that for over 80 percent of this history U.S. laws declared that most of the world's population was ineligible for full American citizenship solely because of race, origins, or gender. In the same manner, for at least two-thirds of its history, the majority of the domestic population in the United States was also ineligible for this political status. The Tocquevillian and post-Tocquevillian theses falter because they center their examinations on the dominant minority in American history—European white men. That is, the relative egalitarianism among white men was surrounded by abundant structured ethno-national hierarchies that accorded all other non-male, non-white, non-Christian, non-heterosexual people an inferior political status. Smith suggests replacing the Tocquevillian perspective with a view of America as having overlapping and multiple traditions so as to be able to pay appropriate attention to oppression and inequality within the United States.

Smith's is not the only criticism of Brubaker's path-breaking 1992 study. Theories of citizenship have been constantly revised to better correspond to real-life situations. The unitary point of view has been criticized in several ways. One is that citizenship is not consistent for each nation-state but highly dependent on internal and external historical developments. According to another, citizenship is not an independent "cultural idiom" but a value contingent on internal and external events.[8] And a third is that citizenship might be coherently defined, but only as the outcome of the political struggle between permanent interest groups (each possessing different conceptions of citizenship).[9] Nevertheless, for all their differences, these still accept the underlying principle that citizenship involves a coherent and stable worldview (at least for particular groups within the state).

Following Brubaker's initial work on citizenship, many scholars chose to explore naturalization as a focal point where the "nature" of citizenship and nationhood is brought into sharp focus. "Admission and exclusion are at the core of communal independence. They suggest the deepest meaning of self-determination."[10] Determining who becomes a member is the state's way of shaping and defining the national community. Thus, granting citizenship is a powerful tool in maintaining the state's sovereignty, especially in times when it confronts substantial external pressures (such as transnational migration), which can undermine its independence and self-determination. However, concentrating only on the inclusion mechanism can be misleading. On the one hand, politicians choose agreed-upon standpoints and "avoid 'compromising' stances, which would mean being of the same mind as the occupants of opposite positions in the space of the political field."[11] The centrality of immigration policies and the vast public attention it draws force politicians to distinguish themselves by using definite and opposing political philosophies. Hence, focusing on incorporation regimes may mislead one to conclude that all policies are coherent and stable. On the other hand, looking only at inclusion does not take into account Walzer's assertion that both admission and exclusion are at the core of communal independence. In this book, I concentrate on the revocation of citizenship in order both to understand why states take away citizenship and to better explain what citizenship is.

Before explaining the reasons for and mechanisms of taking away citizenship, I wish to consider the hegemonic national logic in which modern citizenship is embedded and which constitutes the backdrop for the need to take away citizenship.

The National Logic

As empires disintegrated, the modern states that grew out of them attempted to establish sovereignty over heterogeneous communities and promote an ideology of national homogeneity, persecuting social groups that failed to comply with the unifying ethos. The nation-state typically pursues a tight fit between the perceived ethnic, religious, cultural, or political borders of nationality and its territorial borders. Nationality is constructed around ethnic, religious, cultural, or political identities and by excluding groups that clash with such cohesive factors.

The ideas of nationalism and nations coincide with the arrival of modernity as a powerful order-building system. "Throughout the era of modernity, the nation-state has claimed the right to preside over the distinction between order and chaos, law and lawlessness, citizen and *homo sacer*, belonging and exclusion, useful (=legitimate) product and waste."[12] The nation-state came into being in the eighteenth century in America and Europe, flourished in Europe in the late nineteenth century, and from then on spread to other regions of the world. The modern state signifies the making of a universal legal and constitutional order.[13] A notion was gradually developed arguing that there must be full congruence between institutional-organizational aspects (the state) and cultural aspects (the nation) and among the state framework, society, and the economy.

The national logic divides the whole world into states separated by boundaries. The Western geopolitical imagination endows territorial demarcation with normative significance: the border marks out the sovereignty of each nation-state because the state, the nation, and the border supposedly coincide naturally. The border is also socially significant, creating a dichotomy between the social groups in every nation and thus between "us" and "them."[14] However, the centrality of the nation-state creates a paradox. Although no state exists in which the four elements—society, culture, territory, and government—overlap, most people perceive the world as divided into nation-states. Hence, as a subjective cultural frame, nationalism still provides a political formula for organizing the world.[15] At the same time, the lack of fit is an inbuilt source of instability, and the national order has to be continually reasserted in when the inevitable boundary issues arise.

According to the national logic, loyalty should be exclusive to a single nation-state, and multiple allegiances (or citizenships) should not be allowed. In the case of immigration or border changes, the citizen should choose to which of the two countries to profess his or her complete loyalty. Thus, according to the national logic, a conscious renunciation of citizenship or any act that might imply such a voluntary decision should be grounds for removal of a person's citizenship.

It is important to acknowledge that the current nation-state system is based on the premises of this ideological position. Whether nationalism is addressed as a mode of thought by which people perceive themselves[16] or as a political manipulation generated by interested parties,[17] one can see that the nation-state has become a significant part of human experience, in terms of ideology and everyday life. Most states in the world do not achieve total congruence of the four components of the national idea—society, culture, territory, and government—either because of failures when forming the political unit or because of flaws due to territorial changes, migration and so on, which emerged after sovereignty was achieved. Nevertheless, nationalism today is still perceived as a central cultural frame that is taken for granted. Nation-states have created in their citizens such a profound sense of belonging and identification that their citizens are willing to sacrifice their lives in the name of the state and for its sake.

Citizenship—The Right to Have Rights

The dominance of the national world order in the twentieth century established the possession and acquisition of citizenship as the main path to obtaining rights (practically and theoretically). Although this world order had begun to crystallize in the eighteenth century, it reached its peak only two centuries later, with the nation-state becoming essential to providing a large range of privileges for its citizens. The lack of citizenship signified extreme political exclusion, not only from a specific nation-state, but from the national world order at large.

Arendt argued that, since the nineteenth century, human rights have been exclusively associated with political rights and citizenships. Humans are not equal because of their humanness, but rather become equal citizens under the guarantee of the modern state. "Man, it turns out, can lose all so-called Rights of Man without losing his essential quality as a man, his human dignity. Only the loss of a polity itself expels him from humanity."[18] Hence, stateless people lose all protection from the national order, and are excluded from the sanctuary of the law.

The abhorrent administrations of the authoritarian regimes of the twentieth century seized upon the understanding that rights and privileges are bound up with membership in a sovereign state. For instance, as punishment for fleeing Russia after the Bolshevik Revolution, a decree of December 15, 1922, denationalized the vast majority of Russian refugees who had "voted with their feet" against the Soviet experiment.[19] However, Arendt's argument is reinforced even more extremely by the events of the Holocaust. The "final solution," the extermination of the Jews by the Nazi regime, was "legally" prepared for by depriving Jews of their nationality. First, under the July 14, 1933, Law of the Retraction of Naturalizations and the Derecognition of German Citizenship, non-native-born German Jews lost their citizenship; second, according to new regulations, Jews lost their nationality as soon as they left the borders of the Reich; and lastly according to the 1935 Nuremberg Laws, no Jew could ever be a German citizen. Thus, the deportation of European Jewry to the extermination centers in the East was facilitated by depriving the Jews of any nationality. On one hand, it made the Jews legally stateless and thus external to the responsibility of the national order or any particular nation-state. On the other hand, it contributed to the Nazi propaganda that maintained that the Jews were not properly human.[20] This linkage between citizenship and protection can explain the limited resistance to the Nazi atrocities on the part of local police forces. That is, there was a perception that the state had unrestricted and arbitrary domination over the stateless and refugees.

Adopting Arendt's propositions that human rights are bound to the nation-state, Agamben adds that refugees have nothing but their bare life: "[If refugees] represent such a disquieting element in the order of the nation-state, this is all because by breaking the continuity between man and citizen, nativity and nationality, they put the originary fiction of modern sovereignty in crisis."[21]

Drawing on Agamben's "*homo sacer*" and Arendt's "stateless" people, Bauman[22] claims that refugees and other stateless people are the unintended and unplanned "collateral damage" of the national logic of the political world order. He coined the notion of "human waste" to describe people rejected from the economic and political modern order, a redundant and functionless population. Refugees rendered "naked" from the protection of any nation-state, are perceived by Bauman as an ultimate example of human waste, given that the need for citizenship is fundamental in the modern world.

Of course, there are several important qualifications that have to be made. First, with the advent of human rights and the international institutions that guarantee those rights, the importance of citizenship diminished symbolically and in practice.[23] Second, since the Second World War, the termination of citizenship was usually effectuated in cases where the individual held another citizenship. Thus, instances of expatriation (whether initiated by the state or by the individual) usually did not cause statelessness (see Chapter 4).

In many countries, but not in the United States, there is an explicit provision in the law that forced expatriation cannot be inflicted if it causes statelessness, and even voluntary renunciation of citizenship is not accepted without proof of alternative citizenship.[24] Here the national world order is indeed being enacted to protect the individual. A person wishing to renounce his or her U.S. citizenship must voluntarily and with intent to relinquish U.S. citizenship (1) appear in person before a U.S. consular or diplomatic officer, (2) do so in a foreign country, (3) and sign an oath of renunciation. Renunciation of citizenship does not require acquisition of another nationality.[25] Although the United States warns that this act may result in the citizen becoming stateless, it does not require any assurance that this situation will not occur. Even in cases where the citizen explicitly maintains that he or she does not have any other citizenship, the State Department would approve this renunciation (see Figure 1.1).

BUREAU OF CONSULAR AFFAIRS

CERTIFICATE OF LOSS OF NATIONALITY OF THE UNITED STATES

This form is prescribed by the Secretary of State pursuant to Section 501 of the Act of
October 14, 1940 (54 Stat. 1171) and Section 358 of the Act of June 27, 1952 (66 Stat. 272).

Embassy/Consulate   U.S. Embassy   of the United States of America

at   Bratislava, Slovakia   ss:

I,   Simon R. Hankinson
                            Name

hereby certify that, to the best of my knowledge and belief,

                     Michael Jude GOGULSKI
                            Name

was born at   Phoenix,   AZ
                     Town or City   Province or County

                     U.S.A.   , on   08-08-1972
                     State or Country   Date (mm-dd-yyyy)

DEPARTMENT USE ONLY
CERTIFICATE OF LOSS OF NATIONALITY
APPROVED DEC 16
(Date)
Overseas Citizens Services
DEPARTMENT OF STATE
By

That: he/she never resided in the United States (Dates*)   resided in the U.S.A. until 8/19/2004   ;

That: he/she resides at   resided formerly at 1009 Bradford Drive, Winter Park, FL, U.S.A.   ;

That: he/she acquired the nationality of the United States by virtue of birth in the U.S.A.   ;

That: he/she acquired the nationality of   no other nationality acquired   by virtue of

That: he/she (The action causing expatriation should be set forth succinctly.) renounced his U.S.
citizenship voluntarily for political reasons

That: said expatriating act was performed voluntarily with the intent to relinquish United States citizenship;

That: he/she thereby expatriated him self on (Date)   12-08-2008   under the provisions of
                                                              (mm-dd-yyyy)

Section   349 (a) (5)   of (The Nationality Act of 1940)* (The Immigration and Nationality Act
of 1952 as amended)

That the evidence of such action consists of the following:
DS-4080, Oath of Renunciation signed at the U.S. Embassy Bratislava, Slovakia   ;

That attached to and made a part of this certificate are the following documents or copies thereof:
DS-4080, Oath of Renunciation signed at the U.S. Embassy Bratislava, Slovakia

In testimony whereof, I have hereunto subscribed by name and affixed my office seal this 8th day of

December , 2008
(Month)   (Year)

[SEAL]

                                              Signature

                                              Consul
                                              Title

*Strikeout inapplicable item.

Figure 1.1. Approved Certificate of Loss of Nationality

Research Design

Until now, the issue of revocation of citizenship has been considered from a predominantly legal perspective.[26] Most academic articles have described and assessed the citizenship loss laws or the specific cases where these laws were implemented. That is, legal experts have tried to identify the relationship between those rules or court decisions and other legal resolutions, such as bills, acts, constitutional amendments, international treaties, or other official instruments. The reason is not just stylistic or part of the professional differentiation in respect to other disciplines, but the pragmatic desire to resolve a particular judicial quandary in respect to a specific case. For example, judges will look at the legislative history of a particular law in order to understand the original meaning proposed in the law at the time it was enacted in order to make a better judgment in its current application.

In this book, I place the revocation of citizenship within a sociological framework. That is, I not only compare relevant pieces of legislation with other legislative measures, but also situate the notion of expatriation within its social, political, economic, and historical contexts. Thus, pursuing the example just mentioned, I look at the legislative history of a law, not to understand another legal text, but to learn about the social atmosphere and cultural meanings that were hegemonic at the time the bill was introduced in Congress. One consequence is that we see that single-nation loyalty seems a pressing and even urgent concern in the legislative discourse only at certain times.

This type of sociological analysis has occasionally been utilized by legal scholars. Peter Spiro, for example, looks at citizenship laws to better understand the changing boundaries of the American polity in the face of globalization. Citizenship laws are not just legal documents but texts that can "track the social facts of community membership."[27] Like Spiro, I use U.S. laws, international treaties, consular correspondence, and legislative debates as a lens on American society. But the main question I address is different. Instead of asking who are the "we" or "what are we entitled to receive as citizens?," I ask what are the basic rules to which the notion of citizenship applies.

Like immigration and naturalization policies, policies regarding the loss of citizenship can provide an indication of what constitutes the concepts of citizenship and nationhood. Since "admission and exclusion are at the core of communal independence,"[28] both policies are measures of the nation-state apparatus. However, while the recruitment of new members to the nation-state is basic to cutting-edge research on citizenship, the latter notion of annulment or revocation of citizenship is usually ignored. In order to test the assumption that nation-states revoke the status of citizenship according to their perception of nationhood, I compare the citizenship loss laws and the official debates around them in the United States from its establishment up to the present.

Immigration and the acquisition of a new citizenship evoke strong emotional reactions in that they involve both highly symbolic and institutional transformation. That is to say, becoming an official part of a new community and acquiring new rights and responsibilities accordingly have tremendous effects on new citizens. These changes are especially celebrated in countries that place immigration at the core of their cultural ethos and political considerations. For this reason, the revocation of citizenship in such countries evokes even stronger responses and has greater symbolical importance as it contradicts one of their main legitimizing principles.

Citizenship laws can be seen as texts that are written by the political elite and represent the desired boundaries of the community they govern. In Rogers Smith's terminology, laws that symbolically mark divisions between different nations signify civic ideologies. Additionally, citizenship laws legally incorporate and empower particular groups as distinctive and especially worthy "people." Thus, although revocation of citizenship policies comprises only a small fraction of the entire spectrum of citizenship laws, they can describe the essence of the particular perception of political membership of each state in different contexts.

In studying the legal procedures for the revocation of citizenship, I examine statutory bills, acts, and relevant constitutional amendments, both proposed and legislated; court opinions; proceedings and protocols of commissions regarding the loss of citizenship; consular correspondence, international and bilateral treaties, and debates within the Department of State; and statistical data regarding the implementation of relevant legislative measures. The combination of the various legal proceedings allows me to grasp the different mechanisms and justifications that the United States has implemented in order to denaturalize and denationalize its citizens. I go even deeper by trying to understand the socio-cultural resonance behind such debates. That is, I locate the justifications that state officials (such as members of Congress, consular officers, Supreme Court judges, and diplomats) have used to advocate particular regulations regarding the loss of citizenship.

The empirical data present another theoretical contribution to what is more than a strictly legal discussion of citizenship. From a legal perspective, we should only look at legal texts that have practical implication for the case at hand. Therefore, records of acts that were never legislated, provisions that were not implemented, or sections of the law that go against Supreme Court decisions have little effect on the matter at hand. In this book, I argue that such texts are extremely important from a sociological standpoint. A failed proposal by Congress members during the Civil War for a law regarding forced expatriation of leaders of the Confederacy might not have had any pragmatic consequences for the practice of expatriation, but it does imply that the revocation of citizenship was seen at the time as a culturally legitimate punishment for revolting against the United States. The fact that this law was actually passed by Congress, but was vetoed by President Lincoln, further strengthens this assumption (as discussed in Chapter 2). The same can be argued for proposals for forced expatriation that were made after the use of expatriation as a punishment was declared unconstitutional by the Supreme Court in *Trop v. Dulles* (1958). For example, the fact that the Supreme Court would never agree to involuntary expatriation as suggested in the Patriot Act II (2003) or in Lieberman's Terrorist Expatriation Act (2010) does not mean that those legislative attempts do not matter. Both cases (which will be further considered in Chapter 8) suggest that although the revocation of citizenship is prohibited, it is still considered unobjectionable by some politicians, and it is still legitimate to publicly recommend such practices.[29] Another example can be seen in the provisions regarding forced expatriation and dual citizenship that still remain in the U.S. Code but are not implemented by the State Department. The fact that the provision that citizenship can be stripped away for crimes of treason may not be valid law—and any attempt to implement this provision would be struck down and hence futile—but it does have social and political implications. For one thing, it means that Congress does not perceive such legislation as inappropriate and therefore has not chosen to repeal it. In the oath immigrants have to take upon naturalization, they swear that they "absolutely and entirely renounce and abjure all allegiance and fidelity to any foreign prince, potentate, state, or sovereignty of whom or which I have heretofore been a subject or citizen." Most naturalized citizens do not perform this act and millions of Americans, in fact, do have dual citizenship. There is no doubt that the oath has no practical effect on later renunciations. However, the fact that this part of the oath has never been changed implies that symbolically it still has a function and that the naturalized citizen should ideally transfer his or her national loyalty to the United States upon naturalization.

In the same manner, it is revealing that forced expatriation is not regarded in the same way by the three branches of government. From a legal standpoint, it is of no pragmatic consequence that it took Congress twenty-five years from the time involuntary expatriation was declared unconstitutional to amend many of the grounds for expatriation (see Chapter 3) or that it took the State Department even longer to issue an official memorandum on these grounds (see Chapter 7). However, these delays do have political consequences. They show that the judicial, legislative, and administrative branches are not in sync and have differential understandings of different problems—in this case, whether dual citizenship is allowed and what constitutes intent to lose American citizenship. Thus, there is a separation between the social understandings of official texts and the legal understandings of the same documents.

The data about the laws and legislative debates in the United States about the state's rights to revoke, and citizens' privileges to renounce, citizenship lend support to Rogers Smith's[30] arguments regarding inclusion and citizenship. In formulating expatriation laws, states combined republican, liberal, and ascriptive elements in their deliberations without having any one of the three as a governing principle for debates in the legislature on this issue. Throughout this book, I show that lawmakers consistently legislated expatriation laws in reaction to explicit manifestations of disloyalty (which had various delineations at different times). This, in turn, demonstrates that there is a meta-principle for citizenship that involves the nature of political allegiance. The debates over taking away citizenship have also been also influenced by another issue, which cannot be reduced to any particular citizenship tradition and which is consistent with both positions in the coherence debate—namely, that of maintaining the national order by insisting that dual citizenship should not be allowed. This policy is one of the main principles underlying the need for involuntary expatriation in the world.[31] If citizenship is the legal symbol for belonging to a national community, dual citizenship is a symbol for the existence of multiple national allegiances. The parameters of citizenship are influenced by the political philosophy of the state (such as the definition of disloyal actions or the periodization of expatriation laws). Under the national order, all states and all civic ideals would find dual national loyalty destructive to the sovereignty of the state.

The Terminology of Revoking Citizenship

The practice of termination of citizenship is described in various ways by lawyers, scholars, and laymen. The terms include "expatriation," "denationalization," "denaturalization," "renunciation," and "revocation of citizenship." Although different, these terms utilized to express the loss of citizenship usually indicate an implicit understanding of the meaning of citizenship. In order to avoid limiting myself to one conception of citizenship, I will consider the full spectrum of terms and their implications.

To begin with, although I use the term "expatriation" to describe the phenomenon of loss of citizenship as a whole (for reasons that will be clarified in the course of this discussion of terminology), it usually means a voluntary act of leaving one country for another. Thus, from a literal point of view, it is unclear what exactly a person relinquishes upon expatriation—his or her legal status (citizenship), identity (nationality), allegiance, or residence, or some combination of all four? Therefore, it is not surprising that this term is used differently in different contexts. For example, the common present-day use of the noun "expatriate" designates a person who lives in a foreign county,[32] but Aleinikoff,[33] in his article on the loss of citizenship, applies the same term to a voluntary act of termination of citizenship status. For him, the term "denationalization" refers to a citizen's involuntary termination of citizenship.

Yet "denationalization" does not necessarily refer to the government's act of removing citizenship. If we accept that citizenship is the formal institutionalization of nationality, we will agree that nationalization means formally belonging to a state.[34] However, by limiting the idea of nationality only to established nations, we rule out over 350 groups lacking a sovereign state,[35] such as non-national communities. I doubt that any members of those groups would concur with such a proposition.

The term "denaturalization" is much more specific and thus less disputed. If naturalization is the acquisition of new citizenship, denaturalization means the process by which a non-native citizen loses his or her attained legal status. That is, denaturalization is a provision that revokes a prior judgment of naturalization. Many states have a statute that abrogates a certificate of naturalization if it was illegally obtained, but there have been cases, even in democratic counties such as the United States, in which denaturalization was based on non-democratic grounds. However, use of the term "denaturalization" does not give us information about whether this transformation was initiated by the citizen or by the government, and does not imply a parallel transformation in the individual's self-representation.

Renunciation or relinquishment of citizenship is the voluntary act of requesting permission from the state to terminate the mutual formal relationship. While some individuals wish to terminate any connection with the state for ideological reasons, others might do so in order to avoid fulfilling duties assigned by the state (such as taxes or military service); still others are compelled to relinquish their official status as a precondition for receiving benefits or positions in another country (for example, some countries prohibit dual citizenship, and some employers refuse to hire foreign citizens). Usually, individuals in the latter two categories will terminate only their official relationship with the state but may maintain significant social connections with the land of their former citizenship.

The most common distinction in the loss of citizenship is the one between voluntary and involuntary expatriation. This dichotomy is evident in many government and scholarly papers. For example, in a survey of the citizenship laws of the world,[36] the U.S. government divided loss of citizenship into two categories—voluntary and involuntary loss of citizenship—and made other distinctions (such as native versus naturalized citizens, grounds for expatriation, legal procedures) secondary. Legal experts maintain the two categories to emphasize the importance of intent in the context of the official assessment. Nevertheless, from a sociological standpoint, I would argue that this difference is mainly semantic, and that its usefulness for analysis is questionable. Except for extreme cases of symbolic renunciation on political grounds, the loss of citizenship is usually involuntary in that it is determined by economic, political, and/or social forces outside any individual's control. Despite a philosophical stance that is suspicious of any claim to the possibility for pure individualistic action, I can identify three pragmatic arguments that support the idea that expatriation ultimately is not voluntary. While states may be effectively enforcing the national order of singular citizenship, individuals are prompted by other concerns. First, in many cases, there is a clear economic rationale behind the decision to renounce one's citizenship. This might be to avoid paying taxes, to take up a job in a foreign country, or to reduce bureaucratic hardship—that is, people usually have practical reasons for giving away the rights associated with citizenship. Second, pursuing the line of the first argument, it is questionable whether those people would still expatriate themselves if they could attain their economic desires without giving up their citizenship. As Shklar notes, "The possession of an American passport particularly is profoundly valued, especially by naturalized citizens. Few indeed are the new American citizens who have chosen to throw their naturalization papers away."[37] Moreover, even symbolic renunciation of citizenship is usually performed because of larger political or social pressure. For example, approximately four hundred members of the Black Hebrew community in Israel renounced their American citizenship between 1973 and 1990. Even the U.S. Department of State recognized that this deliberate action was inherently involuntary, in that it was made at the behest of the leadership of this religious cult (see Chapter 7). Lastly, even if an expatriation is truly voluntary, it is questionable whether we, as researchers, can actually establish what the genuine intent behind this decision is. Therefore, in order to avoid assuming true voluntary action, throughout this research I differentiate between state-initiated and privately initiated revocation of citizenship. This distinction reflects a variation in the process of expatriation, rather than a significant category that attributes intentionality to the act.

To sum up, while some researchers or politicians are interested in a particular form of loss of citizenship, this study treats all categories of expatriation as the object of study. In fact, one of the goals of this investigation is to explain the reasons for semantic distinctions and to understand why states are interested in ridding themselves of some of their subjects. The distinctions, together with the notion of expatriation, are intimately tied up with the modern understanding of citizenship.

National Beginnings—American versus British Citizenship

Be it enacted by the Senate and House of Representatives of
the United States of America in Congress assembled, That
any declaration, instruction, opinion, order, or decision
of any officers of this government which denies, restricts,
impairs, or questions the right of expatriation, is hereby
declared inconsistent with the fundamental principles of
this government.
—U.S. Congress, Expatriation Act, 1868

From Subjects to Citizens

In the past, political membership was seen as a biological condition.
Being born into a particular community determined a person's natural
subjectship.[1] Therefore, persons who did acquire allegiance to a new
ruler were considered to be "naturalized," a term that is still used today
although its underlying meaning is usually rejected.[2] Thus, it is common to understand persons in pre-democratic political arrangements
as subjects rather than free citizens. This in turn meant that the world
was divided into groups of people whose allegiance was assigned by
birth, regardless of their color, parentage, or race; consequently, their
political identity was "not alienable: it could not be renounced, abandoned or confiscated."[3] Since one of the debates regarding citizenship
concerns individuals' identity at birth, the history of modern citizenship can be described in terms of the changing relationship between
membership and biology. Before the emergence of the nation-state as
the dominant political arrangement in the nineteenth century, people
were officially bound to each other by hierarchical, overlapping, religious, and dynastic systems. "Legally, people were peasants, gentlemen,
barons, burghers, laity, or clerics first, and Englishmen, Belgians, or
Germans second or third if, at all."[4] A process of separation between
national identity and biology, which began with the political philosophy

of the Enlightenment, crystallized during the French Revolution and in the American Declaration of Independence, deepened throughout the nineteenth and twentieth centuries, and continues even today.[5] But this development has not been linear, equal, or inevitable, for it was introduced in a different context in each country, was actualized differently or even retracted in some, and there are still several countries that grant citizenship only on the basis of ethnic descent. Moreover, this process has never been completed. For most inhabitants of the world, citizenship is still a biological disposition. Most citizens are born into this status and will never abandon it or acquire another. Even those who do change their allegiance and emigrate to another country will do so in relation to a biological trait—family reunification or ethnic homogenization. Most people who have multiple nationalities acquired them by birth. Thus, by asserting that there is a process of separation between national identity and biology, I do not mean to claim that citizenship is in any way divorced from biology, but that there is a growing understanding that citizenship can be attained or lost by individual choice, regardless of biological qualities. The history of expatriation policy in the United States epitomizes this transformation.

The French and the American revolutions, each in its own way, gave the basic form to modern citizenship, one that entailed a repudiation of the natural subjection of people to a particular authoritarian rule.[6] Although French subjects were legally differentiated from foreigners only in the later eighteenth century (as in the *droit d'aubaine* rule relating to inheritance of property), the ideas and practices of French nationality law mutated from absolutist conceptions into a recognizably modern political notion of citizenship.[7] Modern citizenship is based on the rejection of rule by hereditary monarchical and aristocratic families in favor of a broader community of political equals. The French Revolution crystallized the modern institutions of the nation-state and of citizenship. The four aspects of the revolution—the bourgeois revolution, the democratic revolution, the national revolution, and the bureaucratic revolution—led to the form of national citizenship that determines most of men's (and later on women's) obligations and rights up to the present day.[8] The constitution adopted in France in 1791 legally established the term "citizenship" for individuals eligible to call themselves French. In the next century, attitudes toward foreigners in France were constantly changing, in tandem with the changes of political rule. The 1889 Naturalization Law codified for the first time nationality laws according to the *jus soli* principle, which governs French immigration policies till now. This principle states that children born in France can become French citizens upon reaching adulthood.[9] Therefore, citizenship is still determined by biology, but now it is determined by birthplace (in French territory) rather than by descent.

Biological Subjects and Alienable Citizens

But as men, for the atteyning of peace, and conservation of
themselves, have made an Artificial Man, which we call a
Common-wealth; so also have they made Artificial Chains.
—Thomas Hobbes, Leviathan

The above quotation from Thomas Hobbes signifies the beginning of the transformation toward modern political membership. Hobbes' writings illustrate the beginning of Anglo-American liberal thought: He freed the individual to make subjective judgments as to the validity of institutions, and thereby initiated a shift from membership being perceived as a biological condition to membership seen as a social construction.

The independence of the United States formalized a novel approach to the relationship between citizenship and bloodline. In early British common law tradition, legal and political status was associated with the notion of prescribed perpetual allegiance, rather than an idea of citizenship as consensual membership. Allegiances were conceived as natural vertical ties between individual subjects and the king, like parent to child,[10] and these ties could not be dissolved even with the subject's consent. Voluntary renunciation of British subject status was an inconceivable concept. These ties knitted together the British Empire, not only the British nation: "There was no specific citizenship status for the colonies, for Britain itself, or even for the independent Commonwealth countries."[11]

The American concept of citizenship, on the other hand, reflects the continuous tradition of immigration both in its formation and in its myths. Thus, the British colonists' growing unhappiness with British rule arose not only from economic and political frustrations, as presented in the well-known slogan—"no taxation without representation"—but also from grievances regarding the autonomous identity of the settlers. The American War of Independence was fueled by sharp criticisms of the British concept of unchangeable allegiance—an impossible option for the "New World" settlers—and by the adoption of naturalization (or voluntary adhesion to the state) as the principle on which American citizenship was based. In fact, many of the clashes the United States had during the nineteenth century with other countries around the world, including the 1812 war with Great Britain, were connected to the insistence of foreign countries that national allegiance cannot be renounced or transferred.[12] As this book recounts, the United States has lost its progressive edge in this matter, even if its formation initiated moves to less rigid identity between subject and state. Although King George consented to part from the rebellious colonists in the peace treaty after the American Revolution, His Majesty did not perceive this arrangement as a permanent consent for immigrants to freely transfer their allegiance.[13]

From the standpoint of Great Britain and the theory of perpetual allegiance, the main problem of naturalization was not divided national loyalty, but its transfer. Spiro has nicely described this problem: "The British Crown, for instance, would not have cared particularly whether a seaman had in fact transferred his affections to the American Flag. . . . [E]xpatriation represented an intolerable loss of strength to the birth sovereign, in something of a human equivalent of mercantilist paradigms."[14]

Nevertheless, until the American Civil War, it was still pondered whether a person could expatriate himself—that is, relinquish his or her allegiance as an American. In the same manner, it was questionable whether a person could "really" cut his or her allegiance to a country of origin. John Bassett Moore meticulously described the judicial and administrative manifestations of the unclear, and sometimes conflicting, attitudes toward expatriation until the Expatriation Act of 1868, in which expatriation became an explicitly unqualified right in the United States.[15]

An early example of issues surrounding expatriation comes from the end of the nineteenth century. The District court had to rule over citizenship issues in order to assess whether Ballard, Talbot, and Ridick were in violation of the peace treaty with Holland when they captured a Dutch vessel. Edward Ballard, a native-born American citizen renounced his allegiance to Virginia and to the United States in 1794 (under a Virginia statute). However, he did not acquire any other citizenship. The court established that although he expressed his intention of expatriation, the act of the legislature of Virginia did not apply to citizenship in the United States (in which the right of voluntary expatriation was still not recognized). Therefore, Ballard remained a citizen of the United States. In late 1793, Captain Talbot moved to the West Indies and took an oath of allegiance to the French Republic there. Since he did not legally renounce his citizenship in the United States, the court decided that the evidence did not show that Talbot had ceased to be an American citizen. Samuel Ridick, another native citizen of the United States was declared a citizen despite his long residence on a French island, his taking an oath to the French Republic, and his naturalization as a French citizen. Those rulings are very similar to the current understanding of expatriation (see Chapters 6 and 7). Actions that signify expatriation (such as residence abroad for a prolonged period of time, making an oath to another country, and even naturalization in another country) are not sufficient to remove American citizenship. Today's emphasis on intention (albeit provable) has a metaphysical ring to it, which in practice could mean deferring to bureaucratic decisions, more or less flexible in response to the demands (ideological, political, practical) of the moment. However, in the past, the considerations were different. While today the concern is the right of the citizen to remain American as long as he or she does not have intent to relinquish this status, in the past, it was the obligations demanded of the citizen and the rights of the government that were protected. The state's concern with its integrity, and clearly not only territorial integrity, underpins the national world order. In the examples mentioned above, the question of whether Ballard, Talbot, and Ridick, who were captured for illegally fitting out a United States vessel (*L'Ami de la Point-a-Petre*, formerly the *Fairplay*) were American or French, was connected to the question of whether the United States could confiscate the ship or not.

One of the foundational rules regarding naturalization in the United States is the oath of allegiance. Since its introduction in 1795, the oath requires that in order for an immigrant to become a citizen of the United States, he or she has to forswear forever any former national loyalties. Thus, in the first line of the oath, the immigrant declares that he or she does "absolutely and entirely renounce and abjure all allegiance and fidelity to any foreign prince, potentate, state, or sovereignty of whom or which I have heretofore been a subject or citizen." This part of the text is still a mandatory oath for almost all naturalized citizens.[16] Since the oath has never been enforced by American authorities, today this oath is perceived as having only symbolic value. However, in the nineteenth century the oath was certainly taken seriously.[17]

After the Declaration of Independence, the question of how to deal with individuals who did not want to be part of the new allegiance arose. According to the new political ideas of the revolution, allegiance to and membership in a political community were matters of individual choice (and therefore the colonies could lawfully decide to break their allegiance to the British Crown). While the leaders of the revolution believed that the will of the majority was enough for them to extend their jurisdiction over all inhabitants of the freed colonies, many loyalists and patriots questioned the legitimacy of coercing allegiance. How should the new American states treat the dissenting inhabitants—as loyal subjects to Great Britain (and thus as enemies) or as disloyal citizens (and therefore as traitors)? Such charged questions exemplify the national order. A few states initially assumed that upon independence, all inhabitants of the colony owed allegiance to the state. Other states drew on the idea that citizenship should be a contractual relationship and thus specified a time limit (that is, only during a revolutionary situation) for the election of allegiance.[18] Once a person made a choice, he or she could not change his or her mind without risking punishment. The end of the war, and especially the 1783 Treaty of Paris, brought an end to the urgent question of determining the allegiance status of loyalists (as both the security concerns were reduced and loyalists received some protection). After the initial confusion, the United States could commit itself to the right of voluntary expatriation.[19]

One of the solutions was a speech act. A loyalist who wanted to clear his or her name (and protect him- or herself from being sent off to Europe) could do so simply by renouncing allegiance to George III alongside taking an oath of allegiance to the United States. In contrast to the British ideal of perpetual allegiance, a statement that signified intent to renounce citizenship had weight in the United States.[20] We will later see that words have not been the only or main method of expressing expatriation. But, by the end of the twentieth century, speech acts had come to be the (almost) exclusive benchmark to profess intent to relinquish American citizenship.

This is not to say that the oath of allegiance was always taken seriously. Even in the first years of national independence, some questioned whether it was really a sufficient measure of intent to become exclusively American. Harris Otis, a Federalist lawyer from Boston, maintained that "A Frenchman is a Frenchman everywhere. . . . [T]hough he may take his naturalization oath in this country, it does not alter his character."[21] Different views of the bond between individual and a birth nation-state and an adopted country, contractual and essentialist, are here superimposed, and do not yield to a narrative of progressive development.

The standpoint of the executive branch was mostly that foreigners could abjure their former allegiance to become Americans. Thomas Jefferson, while serving as the first secretary of state under George Washington (1790–1793), maintained that "Our citizens are certainly free to divest themselves of that character by emigration and other acts manifesting their intention, and may then become the subjects of another power, and free to do whatever the subjects of that power may do."[22] Voluntary expatriation was accepted and even celebrated as a unique contribution of American political philosophy. However, as the legal and administrative evidence suggests, it was not clear what constituted intent for renunciation. Should the oath to another political power be taken as a definite indication of the desire to relinquish American citizenship? Or, do expatriation acts such as residence or naturalization in another country sufficiently signify intent? Situated readings of the arguably philosophical notion of intent, and that of a speech act, or of actions without words to define them, bear on the maintenance of the national world order.

Prior to 1868, the courts of the United States generally accepted that the right of voluntary expatriation was not absolute and that a citizen could not renounce his allegiance to the United States without the permission of the government. The rule was that naturalization in a foreign country did not necessarily release a person from his former national allegiance. In *Talbot v. Janson* (1795), it was argued that naturalization in another country did not represent the renunciation of American citizenship.[23] Only when James Buchanan took office as the secretary of state in 1845 was it explicitly and formally declared that there is an unqualified right of voluntary expatriation and that naturalization releases the individual from his or her obligation to the former sovereign. When Buchanan became president in 1857, this policy was reasserted. Of course, one needs to remember that the administration usually perceived the issue in terms of obstacles a foreigner faced in becoming American, not in terms of Americans who wished to divest themselves of their American citizenship.[24]

In 1868, a series of events led the United States to officially recognize the right of Americans to expatriate themselves. Congress, in an "Act Concerning Rights of American Citizens in Foreign States" (HR 768), which later would be called the Expatriation Act, legislated, for the first time, the original American principle of transferable allegiance. *"Be it enacted by the Senate and House of Representatives of the United States of America in Congress assembled,* That any declaration, instruction, opinion, order, or decision of any officers of this government which denies, restricts, impairs, or questions the right of expatriation, is hereby declared inconsistent with the fundamental principles of this government."[25] In Chapter 4, we will see that that legislative measure coincided with diplomatic attempts to regulate the same standard. This act led President Ulysses S. Grant to say in his State of the Union speech (1873) that the United States had "led the way in the overthrow of the feudal doctrine of perpetual allegiance."[26]

In 1866, the State Department learned that a number of naturalized citizens had been arrested in Ireland. These included several naturalized Americans who had joined the Fenian movement to fight for Irish independence and who were captured and put on trial. Notable among these individuals were Captain John Warren and Augustine E. Costello, who were tried for treason on account of participation in the Jacmel expedition, an attempt to supply arms to the Irish uprising.[27] During his trial, Captain John Warren maintained that he could not be tried for treason because he was an American citizen and owed no loyalty to Britain. The British however, maintained that being native-born in Ireland, he was subject to procedures and punishments that properly applied only to British subjects, not to aliens. Initially, the United States tried diplomatically to assert its right to naturalize citizens; but in 1868

Congress had had enough. Therefore, it passed the Expatriation Act of 1868, formally declaring for the first time the right of expatriation from another country to the United States.

Since the ideal of transferable allegiance was inherent to American political ideology and was usually supported by the judicial and administrative branches of U.S. government, the 1868 Expatriation Act was primarily an assertive international statement. Congressman Nathaniel Banks (MA-R), who introduced the bill, maintained that "The time, Mr. Speaker, has come when the American Government should assert its principles." Moreover, in the third section of the bill, it was enacted that in the case of naturalized Americans who were arrested as foreign nationals, the president was authorized to use any means (not amounting to war) to obtain their release. In keeping with this idea, the Foreign Affairs Committee was suggested a doctrine of reprisals—that is, a policy of arresting subjects of other nations until the American prisoners in those countries were treated as American citizens.

The insistence on perpetual allegiance of the subjects, released only by the sovereign himself, ceased to exist at the beginning of the twentieth century in most of the world. This meant that citizenship was transferable. "Nations came to recognize that this medieval notion no longer fit the needs of a globe where rail and steamship travel, coupled with the dislocations of the industrial revolution, led to massive flows of permanent migration."[28] Nevertheless, we will see that while an individual could switch from one national belonging to another, until recently, the same individual could not retain both of his or her citizenships. In other words, citizenship was expected to be singular.

Alexander Hamilton nicely expressed the notion of exclusive nationality which was hegemonic at the time. "A dispassionate and virtuous citizen . . . will scorn to stand on any but purely American ground. . . . To speak figuratively, he will regard his own country as a wife to whom he is bound to be exclusively faithful and affectionate. And he will watch with a jealous attention every propensity of his heart to wander towards a foreign country, which he will regard as a mistress that may pervert his fidelity and mar his happiness."[29] In order to regulate this single allegiance, the United States began to compel the expatriation of Americans who displayed indications that they had transferred their national loyalty.

Only with the Fourteenth Amendment and Expatriation Act of 1868, could a citizen officially choose to rescind his American citizenship. As the perception of citizenship became disconnected from the assumption of unconditional allegiance, the opposite also became conceivable— namely, that the state had an option to terminate the political status of citizens for lack of allegiance. In other words, the state had the power to revoke citizenship from persons who were not entitled (from the perspective of Congress) to be members of the polity anymore. This judicial transformation follows Hobbes' proposition that according to enlightenment principles the state can expatriate its citizens. Namely, "If a Soveraign Banish his Subject; during the Banishment, he is not Subject."[30]

In the new formulation of the relationship between the individual and the state, belonging to any political community was conditional upon the actions of the individual. Expatriation or banishment would lead to the discontinuation of the mutual obligations and responsibilities of the state and the subject.[31] This assumption that Congress has the authority to divest an American citizen of this status will be discussed in the following chapter.

3

Legislative Initiatives

Mr. Speaker, we have approximately 25,000 Japanese interned in our state, and no one could be more interested in this legislation than I, because we are very much concerned that some of these people may be left there to mingle with our people when this war has been completed.
—Congressman Richard Harless (D-AZ), 1944

Congress deliberated on the issue of forced expatriation twice before the American Civil War. The first time was during the debates on the original Thirteenth Amendment (1810); the second was in reaction to the unacceptable betrayal on the part of the Confederacy (from the standpoint of the Union). Both proposals were passed by Congress but were never enacted into law. However, from the end of the nineteenth century until the mid- twentieth century, the legislative branch initiated and legislated many expatriation laws. The hegemonic perception of Congress was that citizenship can and should be taken away if the American citizen acquires another nationality or commits certain acts that represent a transfer of allegiance. Only in the late 1950s did Congress begin to question this policy (mainly in conjunction with new rulings by the Supreme Court). Analyzing debates in the two houses of Congress has important implications for understanding policies and public opinion. The purpose of this chapter is not just to survey the legislative history of U.S. expatriation law[1] but to chart the pattern of difference between the official language of the law and the socio-cultural context in which expatriation laws were legislated in the United States. I show that legislation and debates in Congress regarding the practice of taking away citizenship were mainly introduced to eliminate dual citizenship.

The Original Thirteenth Amendment

In 1810 Congress debated whether to add another amendment to the Constitution that would strip American citizenship from citizens who acquire any title of nobility from another country. According to Article 5 of the Constitution, for an amendment to pass, the proposal has to receive a two-thirds majority in both houses and receive ratification by three-fourths of the states. The Titles of Nobility Amendment (TONA) was approved by the Senate by a vote of 19 to 5 on April 27, 1810. The House of Representatives then approved the amendment on May 1, 1810, by a vote of 87 to 3, and TONA was submitted to the states for ratification. The text reads as follows:

> If any citizen of the United States shall accept, claim, receive or retain, any title of nobility or honour, or shall, without the consent of Congress, accept and retain any present, pension, office or emolument of any kind whatever, from any emperor, king, prince or foreign power, such person shall cease to be a citizen of the United States, and shall be incapable of holding any office of trust or profit under them, or either of them.[2]

The reasons for proposing this amendment are obscure, and there are no records of the debates on it. Some scholars have suggested that it was introduced in reaction to partisan politics or xenophobia. Others have argued that it was connected to rising fears, during the decade preceding the War of 1812, that the United States would be recaptured and marginalized by European powers and that it also stemmed from the long tradition of opposition to hereditary privilege in the United States.[3]

The passage of an amendment of this nature would have had the potential to denationalize many Americans and even to change the course of history. For example, most lawyers could have been under threat of losing American citizenship for taking the title of "Esquire." Moreover, some of the American "founding fathers" such as George Washington, Alexander Hamilton, and James Madison had received honorary titles from France.[4] This amendment would have put them outside the pale of legitimate American-ness. In the end, an insufficient number of states ratified the Titles of Nobility Amendment so that it did not become part of the Constitution, though ratification by only one more state would have given TONA the three-fourths approval (13 of 17) required.[5]

This failed amendment was briefly discussed in the Supreme Court in relation to expatriation. In *Afroyim v. Rusk* (1967) the judges gave some consideration to whether this proposal should have any implication for the then-current interpretation of forced expatriation. It was argued that "this 'obscure enterprise' in 1810, motivated by now discredited constitutional premises, cannot offer any significant guidance for solution of the important issues now before us."[6]

Expatriation and the American Civil War

Although never implemented, the possibility of revoking American citizenship as a punishment was proposed during the American Civil War (1861–1865). On July 2, 1864, Senator Benjamin Wade (R-OH) and Representative Henry Winter Davis (R-NY) introduced a Reconstruction Bill (HR 244). Congress was concerned that President Lincoln's "10 percent plan" for reincorporating Southern states into the Union was too weak. While Lincoln was willing to embrace any Confederate state in which 10 percent of its voters swore loyalty to the United States, the Wade-Davis Bill demanded extreme measures from these formerly rebellious states—such as a loyalty oath taken by 50 percent of the white males, abolition of slavery (but not suffrage for the new freedmen), appointment of provisional military governors in the seceded states, disqualification of Confederate officials from voting or holding office, and the revocation of citizenship from the leaders of the rebellion (see Figure 3.1). Although the bill was passed by Congress, these regulations were viewed by many as degrading and unrealistic. Eventually, President Lincoln pocket-vetoed[7] the bill because he believed it weakened the efforts to win the war and secure emancipation. In particular, the bill would have compelled him to repudiate the new government of Louisiana. The debates around this bill dealt with Southern reconstruction and did not include any discussion of the theoretical or actual implications of expatriation practices.

In the end, both the Wade-Davis Bill and the Titles of Nobility Amendment did not become law, but in neither case was the issue of expatriation connected to the final decision to abandon the laws. This may suggest that even before the American Civil War, the idea of force-fully disconnecting the tie between the individual and the state was seen as a legitimate punishment for Americans who had transferred their allegiance.

The first occasion on which the revocation of citizenship was introduced and actually performed was during the Civil War, when the 38th Congress (1864–1865) decided to take this step. The overwhelming extent of desertion from the Confederacy and the regiments of the North had significant implications for the social cohesion of both armies (and played an important role in the ultimate failure of the South). In contrast to the horrendous penalties meted out to Confederate deserters, the North tried to delineate a tough but "humane" form of punishment. Section 21 (copied from Bill 175 passed by the Senate) of the Enrollment Act (HR 678) imposed a penalty of citizenship rights revocation for future deserters, as well as current deserters who did not return to their post within sixty days. This section was introduced as part of a bill that provided authority to call for and regulate additional manpower for the national forces. Most of the debates concerning this bill dealt with the relative power of Congress over American citizens, rather than the meaning of this citizenship (or its revocation). When Congressman Andrew J. Rogers (D-NJ) opposed the proposed bill, he was not concerned about the changing value of citizenship; instead, he feared that the bill's provisions would impose an unnecessary burden on the citizens of the United States. Others, like Congressman John W. Chanler (D-NY), argued that this proposed law would increase the tyrannical powers of presidents. Congressmen James F. Wilson (R-IA), James C. Allen (D-IL), and Philip Johnson (D-PA), who opposed the bill on the grounds that it inflicted punishment without due process, pointed out that there would be no tribunal that decided upon this punishment, and that taking away citizenship from current deserters constituted a retroactive punishment (that is, the bill proposed inflicting punishment on deserters who deserted before the passage of the law). Nevertheless, the legislation was passed and became effective on March 3, 1865. The objections to the revocation of citizenship were connected to the mechanism of the penal system or were part of the protests against the Civil War itself.

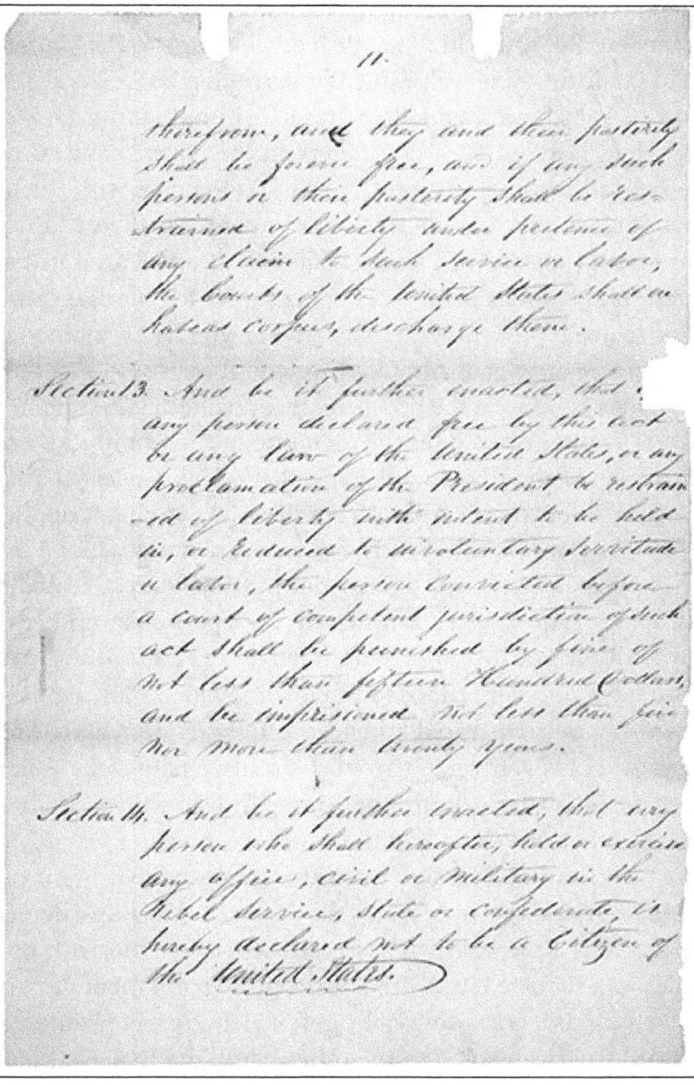
11.

therefrom, and they and their posterity shall be forever free, and if any such persons or their posterity shall be restrained of liberty under pretence of any claim to such service or labor, the courts of the United States shall on habeas corpus, discharge them.

Section 13. And be it further enacted, that any person declared free by this act or any law of the United States, or any proclamation of the President be restrained of liberty with intent to be held in, or reduced to involuntary servitude or labor, the person convicted before a court of competent jurisdiction of such act shall be punished by fine of not less than fifteen Hundred Dollars, and be imprisoned not less than five nor more than twenty years.

Section 14. And be it further enacted, that every person who shall hereafter, hold or exercise any office, civil or military in the Rebel service, State or Confederate, is hereby declared not to be a Citizen of the United States.

Figure 3.1. The Wade-Davis Bill. The original draft of Section 14 of the Wade-Davis Bill revokes citizenship from all participants, civil or military, in the rebellion against the United States. When the bill was presented to Congress, this section was played down, and the proposal was to punish only the leaders of the Confederate rebellion (above the grade of colonel). Handwritten copy of the Wade-Davis Bill as originally submitted in 1864 (Records of Legislative Proceedings; Records of the United States House of Representatives 1789–1946; Record Group 233; National Archives).

Two years later, the provision that revoked the citizenship of deserters was amended. Bill 108 held that enlisted volunteers to the United States who had "faithfully" served until the surrender of Lee and Johnston on April 19, 1865, and then left the ranks without authority, assuming that they had fulfilled their contract with the government, would not forfeit their citizenship as deserters. As was the case with the original bill (HR 678), the opposition to this argument was divorced from any general perception of American nationality. It was feared instead that the amendment would present an opportunity for thousands of "real" deserters to avoid punishment; that soldiers who had remained in their ranks would be outraged; and that this would impose a greater burden on the taxpayers. In 1912, the provision that revoked citizenship from deserters was further relaxed. At the direction of the Committee on Naval Affairs, Congressman Lemuel P. Padgett (D-TN) suggested amending the law that stripped citizenship from deserters so that it applied only during times of war (HR 17483). The debates did not question the meanings or implications of losing citizenship, but considered only whether it was the appropriate judicial punishment for a particular crime.

Only with the Fourteenth Amendment and Expatriation Act of 1868 could a citizen officially choose to follow the Hobbesian assertion that allegiance can be transferred and accordingly renounce his American citizenship. However, once the idea of citizenship was potentially divorced from birthplace, the nation-state was able to demand the reverse. In other words, it had the power to revoke citizenship from persons who did not deserve (from the congressional point of view) to be members of the polity any more. Both decisions determined that citizenship was a basic right for any American but with opposing rationales. On the one hand, the Fourteenth Amendment declares that U.S. citizenship is a constitutional right, which is granted automatically at birth on American soil. On the other hand, the Expatriation Act of 1868 declared the right of all to change their allegiance. The latter law reflects more than any other law the contractual principle behind the liberal ethos of the United States, and posits that because the relationship between the American individual and the state is contractual, it can be terminated at any point by the will of the citizen. While today the right of expatriation may appear natural and trivial, this was not always the case. In the past, and in some countries even today, the state strictly defended its gates from any attempt to shirk civil or military obligations by running away.

The Progressive Era

The legislation that has been produced since the Expatriation Act of 1868 reflects the beginning of a different attitude regarding the perceived relationship between the citizen and the state. The Expatriation Act of 1907, which was legislated in response to the anxiety regarding high levels of immigration, was the first statute to specify acts of expatriation. Among the actions in this statute (HR 24122) that are cause for punishment by expatriation are taking an oath of allegiance to a foreign government; being naturalized by a foreign government; establishing residence abroad by a naturalized American citizen who lives for two years in his native country; and, for women, marrying a foreigner (even if they continue to reside in the United States). Beforehand, such acts could have caused the loss of citizenship, not through law but according to the various treaties the United States had signed with particular states.[8] Moreover—and this provision would have important implications during the Second World War—"no American citizen shall be allowed to expatriate himself when this country is at war." The multiplication of reasons for expatriation meant an elaboration and "internalization" of the national world order.

Although the Expatriation Act of 1907 did not necessarily conform to the philosophy of the Progressive movement, it was the major Progressive Era federal law affecting women's citizenship.[9] Developed in reaction to fears that alien men married American women simply to get a foothold in the United States, this law designated marriages between American women and foreign citizens as acts of voluntary expatriation. Therefore the 1907 Expatriation Act was sometimes termed the "Gigolo Act." This act was a tremendous setback for women's struggle for full citizenship rights, as it implied that women derived their status as citizens from their American husbands rather than from their own individuality. This standpoint on gender relations, in which family ties are stronger than nationality bonds, was not unusual at the time, and many countries had similar provisions in their law books. Thus, this law received much criticism from major women's political organizations, especially those that were struggling to secure voting rights for women. Although their grievances were introduced to Congress in the 1910s, only after the passage of the Nineteenth Amendment, which secured women's suffrage, did organized women move to challenge directly the gendered provision in the 1907 law. The 1907 act was repealed in 1922.

Hobbes saw women's oppression as contractual rather than biological.[10] "And whereas some have attributed the Dominion to the Men onely, as being of the more excellent Sex; they misreckon it. For there is not always that difference of strength, or prudence between the man and the woman."[11] Nevertheless, patriarchy-based citizenship ended only when the Gigolo Act was repealed, 271 years after Hobbes' assertion, and the Cable Act (sponsored by John Cable, R-OH) allowing a woman who married a foreigner to retain her American citizenship was passed. However the new law did not fully repeal the idea that women's citizenship is dependent upon marriage. First, the Cable Act specified that a woman who lived for two years in her husband's country would lose her nationality. Second, women also lost their citizenship upon marriage to foreigners who were not eligible for citizenship. The law was mostly directed toward Asians, although anarchists and polygamists were also a focus.[12] In a series of amendments (1930, 1931, and 1934), those sexual and racial discriminations were abolished, not without direct pressure from women and Chinese Americans.

Considering the tremendous symbolic effect the 1907 act had on women's conception as full citizens in America, and in contrast to the Naturalization Act of 1906,[13] the 1907 act was debated publicly in Congress for only a short time. James Breck Perkins (R-NY), who was the main advocate for the Gigolo Act, convinced those objecting to the bill that the section on women was already law and that the new legislation only conferred on women the right to regain their American citizenship after the termination of marriage. In her analysis of the Expatriation Act of 1907, Nicolosi has convincingly argued that "in addition to helping to adjust foreign policy, codified derivative citizenship provided an additional function for the state: a penalty for American women who married foreign men . . . especially racially ineligible [for citizenship] foreigners."[14] This act was also passed in the Senate without any debate except over a few technical corrections to the text of the bill. Although the family is an essential unit in national ideologies, it appeared here as a threat to the order of singular nationalities.

On April 25, 1933, the Committee on Immigration was designated by President Franklin D. Roosevelt to review the nationality laws and practices of the United States, to recommend revisions, and to codify one comprehensive nationality law. After seven years of work, the committee introduced HR 6680 (named the "codification of the nationality laws of the United States," or the Nationality Act of 1940) in the House of Representatives. The bill itself was passed unanimously by the committee and was endorsed by the Departments of State, Justice, Labor, and War, by the navy, the president, and the attorney general, and by the American Bar Association. Along with such wide-ranging approval of the bill, and given the fact that it was presented as simply a codification of existing immigration laws in a context of collective dedication to complying with the war efforts during the Second World War, it was not surprising that there was not much debate on the law.

The Nationality Act of 1940 dealt with issues of immigration that were not necessarily connected to the war in Europe. And although the United States had yet to enter the Second World War, the winds of war had crossed the Atlantic Ocean. Several times during the discussions regarding the bill, the notion that the United States was under a state of emergency was brought up. The drafters of the law emphasized that the secretary of state, the secretary of the navy, and the secretary of war approved this bill. Louis Johnson, the acting secretary of war, mentioned the War Department's special interest in section 402, which dealt with the presumption of expatriation for Americans who lived abroad and thus requested "expediting the passage of the bill in question, in the interests of national defense."Mr. Samuel Dickstein (D-NY) explained that "this proposed legislation will not only be materially beneficial to the country in the future, but particularly so at this time of disturbance and agitation by 'fifth columnists' and other subversive groups." Mr. Edward Rees (R-KS) added that "Under this bill, we believe we have covered the question of fascism, nazi-ism, communism, or any other 'ism,' although they are not specifically mentioned by name."[15] Dual citizenship was seen not only as an administrative problem, but as a security problem.

Although Bill 6680 contained 98 pages, followed by a report of 164 pages, it was almost uncontested and unamended on the floor (except for several technical changes in the wording of the law). Most congressmen who participated in the discussion on the Nationality Law utilized their time to congratulate themselves and praise the hard work of constructing a unified law regarding immigration and naturalization.

Nevertheless, the Nationality Act of 1940 did include "new" policies and considerably extended the list of acts that were interpreted as causes for expatriation. For the first time, this list included actions that did not involve the assumption of a new nationality. These expatriation acts were part of the State Department mind-set, but were not officially legislated by Congress. According to this legislation, a native-born or a naturalized citizen would lose his or her American citizenship by entering or serving in a foreign military; taking foreign employment under certain circumstances; voting in a foreign election; formally renouncing citizenship; being convicted of any act of treason; bearing arms against the United States; attempting to overthrow the government by force; or deserting during wartime. In addition naturalized citizens would lose their citizenship if they resided in another country for five years (or three years in their native country). The motive for such legislation by a liberal administration could be explained by the anticipation of war and the concern that German Americans might have dual loyalty. In a similar vein, an act of September 27, 1944, established that remaining outside the United States for the purpose of avoiding military service would be considered grounds for loss of citizenship.

The Second World War

The act of July 1, 1944 (HR 4103), removed the restriction on renunciation of American citizenship within the borders of the United States (or any of its outlying possessions) in time of war. The appearance of this amendment simply as a bureaucratic correction has caused legal scholars surveying expatriation laws to ignore its existence or to underestimate its importance.[16] However, close analysis of the debates on this amendment reveal one of the darkest hours in American domestic history. Following this legislation, 5,589 American citizens of Japanese descent renounced their citizenship. Since they were incarcerated in concentration camps without any hearing or trial, following decades of social discrimination, this renunciation can hardly be considered voluntary.[17] The nominal generality of the law was intended to obscure the specific aim of its legislators—namely, to find and establish a measure that would enable the American government to expatriate and deport as many native-born American citizens of Japanese descent as possible without interference by the Supreme Court. Thus, in Congress it was explicitly argued that "while the bill is general, it has been discussed with reference to the Japanese. We in the West understand the Japanese problem" (Congressman Leroy J. Johnson R-CA); "As a matter of fact, this bill is intended primarily and 100 percent for the Japanese" (Congressman Thomas Rolph R-CA). Similarly, Congressman Charles A. Halleck (R-IN) was concerned about "the all-inclusive provisions of this bill," which could potentially hurt non-Japanese citizens.[18] This resolution was passed unanimously in the Immigration and Nationalization Committee and by a vast majority in the House (111 ayes versus 33 nays).[19]

Many of the objections to the law, mainly by the representatives from California (where most Japanese Americans resided), involved complaints that the law was not drastic enough and thus would not attain its original racist goal. Accordingly, Congressman Leroy J. Johnson (R-CA) suggested amending this bill in order to denationalize more Japanese Americans, by not limiting the act of renunciation to writing or signature on governmental forms and only for the duration of the war. This suggested modification raised criticism from some congressmen, who sympathized with the objection to the revision, but feared that it would have unintended consequences for other segments of the American people. In the words of Congressman Richard Harless (D-AZ), "Mr. Speaker, we have approximately 25,000 Japanese interned in our state, and no one could be more interested in this legislation than I, because we are very much concerned that some of these people may be left there to mingle with our people when this war has been completed . . . but let us not be so stupid as to pass legislation which may be declared unconstitutional."[20] This line of reasoning, which repeated itself several times during the debate by various congressmen from both parties, illustrates nicely that this legislation had a racist undertone in addition to its reflecting republican anxiety due to the ongoing war. First, many congressmen who initially distinguished between loyal and disloyal Japanese dropped the use of this distinction as the debate became tempestuous and expressed a desire to get rid of all Japanese Americans. Second, some congressmen expressed the need to deal with the "Japanese question" on the grounds that Japan interfered with American life, economy, and values even after the termination of the war (Thomas Rolph, R-CA, and Johnson, R-CA). Third, while many congressmen wanted to legislate an even harsher law against the Japanese population in America, the foremost objection was that it might be ruled unconstitutional, rather than that it was essentially unconstitutional or morally wrong (Herman P. Eberharter, D-PA, Samuel Dickstein, D-NY, Asa L. Allen, D-LA). Lastly, the discussion centered mainly on the disloyal Japanese rather than including American citizens of German or Italian descent (Charles A. Hallek, R-IN, Edward Rees, R-KS).

Racial prejudice against Japanese Americans during the Second World War was not limited to efforts to revoke their citizenship. Whether we use the euphemism of "relocation centers" coined by the War Relocation Authority (WRA) or the more analytic but harsh term of "concentration camps," there is no doubt that the internment of thousands of Japanese Americans during the Second World War is one of the most appalling episodes in American domestic history. Although those policies were justified as necessary war-time preventive measures, both the incarceration and expatriation of Americans of Japanese descent are tainted by racial bias, especially compared to the lack of any formal collective exclusion of American citizens of German or Italian descent. Racism, a more essentialist viewpoint, was enlisted to help define American nationality, with its contractual roots in becoming a home to colonists and immigrants.

The Cold War

The next act of legislation regarding the loss of citizenship took place during the "second red scare," or the McCarthy era, in the United States. The Immigration and Nationality Act of 1952 brought together into a single statute all legislation regarding immigration and nationality. Although most of its provisions had been enacted in previous legislation, it did introduce novel segments of the law that strengthened and tightened the requirements for citizenship and its loss. This act ended the blanket exclusion of immigrants based on race, only to replace it with a "rigid immigration quota system based on national origins and racial categories."[21] The Immigration and Nationality Act of 1952 also extended the possible grounds for expatriation to include foreign government employment if it required a declaration of allegiance. In addition, this law allowed the government to deport immigrants or naturalized citizens engaged in subversive, especially allegedly communist, activities. The communist threat could be connected to a security threat from the Soviet Union, to the enforcement of domestic order in relation to American Trotskyists, or to the conceptual threat to the national world order. And indeed, Marxism does postulate and promote bonding across nationalities in a manner that which can be seen to be opposed to the national world order with its demands for singular allegiance.

The Expatriation Act of 1954 determined that nationality was to be lost upon criminal conviction for the violation of the Smith Act (1940),[22] which, although it predated McCarthyism, was enlisted to prosecute Communist Party supporters and leaders. In contrast to the Immigration and Nationality Act of 1952, the 1954 act extended the threat of expatriation and deportation beyond immigrants and naturalized citizens to include native-born Americans as well. President Dwight D. Eisenhower's State of the Union address (January 7, 1954) included a specific request that Congress enact a law that would revoke American citizenship from Communists:

> The subversive character of the Communist Party in the United States has been clearly demonstrated in many ways, including court proceedings. We should recognize by law a fact that is plain to all thoughtful citizens— that we are dealing here with actions akin to treason—that when a citizen knowingly participates in the Communist conspiracy he no longer holds allegiance to the United States. I recommend that Congress enact a legislation to provide that a citizen of the United States who is convicted in the courts of hereafter conspiring to advocate the overthrow of this government by force or violence be treated as having, by such act, renounced his allegiance to the United States and forfeited his United States citizenship.[23]

Following this speech, several bills containing additional grounds for expatriation were introduced in the Committee on the Judiciary.

On July 21, 1954, HR 7130, which proposed stripping citizenship from Americans who commit any act of treason according to sections 2383, 2384, and 2385 (the Smith Act) of Title 18 (Crimes and Criminal Procedure) in the U.S. Code, was introduced in the House. The motion to suspend the rules[24] on the deliberation of this bill encountered no objections (except from Congressman Michael A. Feighan, D-OH, who complained that his own proposed bill 7265, which expanded even further the list of crimes punishable by the loss of citizenship, was not endorsed by the Judiciary Committee), and after a few speeches by congressmen, the Expatriation Act of 1954 was passed with the necessary two-thirds majority. The vast bipartisan support stemmed from the fact that the idea for the bill was suggested by the president and that it was concerned with the United States' greatest fear at that time—Communism. In the Senate, the same bill received one objection. Senator McCarran (D-NV) argued forcefully against it, stating that "Depriving a felon of his civil rights is, of course, an accepted thing; but depriving a felon of his citizenship, which means his basic nationality, is an entirely different matter" and this should not be done easily.[25] Moreover, he argued that this bill would not be fighting Communism effectively and was clearly unconstitutional. Nevertheless, his actual amendment was essentially technical (inserting the word "willfully" into the provision) and thus was accepted with no counterargument by either the Senate or the House. Although many of the grounds for expatriation have been withdrawn over the years, and although such provisions would be nullified under *Trop v. Dulles* (1958; discussed in Chapter 6), stripping away citizenship for crimes of treason still remains unchanged on the books.

Since the passage of the Expatriation Act of 1954, Congress has not initiated new acts with additional grounds for expatriation. Moreover, over the years, the Supreme Court has overturned many of the previous grounds for the revocation of citizenship as unconstitutional.[26] Following the courts, Congress repealed the provisions that revoked citizenship for draft evasion (1976), desertion (1978), voting in a foreign country (1978), the 1952 addition to the subversion principle (1982), and residence abroad (1994). Those legal changes, the cultural transformation, and the current situation regarding both expatriation and multiple allegiances will be the focus of the next section.

Citizenship and Expatriation

The two sides of the citizenship coherence debate (described in Chapter 1) disagree about whether citizenship is a coherent and stable concept, or a mixture of indistinct policies and ideological positions. In accordance with Brubaker's perception of citizenship, we would expect that the United States would have stable, consistent, liberal, or ethnic laws of expatriation. Alternatively, as suggested by Smith, we should see an irregular mixture of republican, liberal, and ethnic expatriation laws.

In formulating expatriation laws, the U.S. government has combined republican, liberal, and ethnic elements in its deliberations without having any one of the three as a dominant principle for congressional debates on this issue. In most cases, the need to solve a particular quandary laid the groundwork for stripping away citizenship rather than an ideological predisposition or principle pertaining to questions such as, Who should be an American? What is the relation between the individual and the state? Can citizenship be taken away? It seems that the appearance of allegiance has played a greater role in the creation of expatriation laws than coherent viewpoints. Rogers Smith describes American citizenship regulation in a similar way: "American citizenship laws have always emerged as none too coherent compromises among the distinct mixes of civic conceptions advanced by the more powerful actors in different eras."[27] Smith argues that this combination is constructed as a means to gain popularity and political endorsement without any constant underlying guiding principle. Indeed, expatriation laws do not follow any strict republican, liberal, or ethnic principle but consistently react to the visible manifestation of massive disloyalty (which has had various delineations at different times).

Academic literature covering debates in Congress as well as media reports have tended to assume that the debates reflected the conventional division between Republicans and Democrats, majority versus minority, and were therefore inconsequential. According to this bipolar paradigm, the debates on expatriation laws would reflect the constructed division between the two parties. But senators and representatives from both sides of the political divide have advocated the need to revoke citizenship from certain people at certain periods with no overt distinction between them in this regard. It is true that usually the administration has been able to enforce its viewpoint on the entire Congress. However, this has happened under both liberal and conservative presidents. Moreover, most bills have been introduced in Congress after they had been unanimously adopted by both Republicans and Democrats in the relevant committees.

Scholars of citizenship studies have usually equated the ideas of citizenship and immigration policies. Consequently, citizenship laws have tended to be seen as regularly associated with immigration patterns. From this standpoint, the introduction of new expatriation laws should correspond to changes in the number of people entering the United States. However, Figure 3.2 shows that even if one can discover a relation between the number of immigrants entering the United States and the numbers of laws dealing with expatriation (perhaps a positive relation until the 1920s or a negative association from the 1950s until today), it is evident that there is no constant relationship between these two variables.

If any pattern can be found, it is not in an overarching philosophy of political membership or party politics. The key factor instead is associated with periods of armed conflict and (real or imagined) threat to the country. The introduction of most bills has occurred in response to events that generated fear for the existence of the United States as an independent state. That is, while the substance of expatriation laws is purely political, the introduction of these laws follows periods of armed conflict. The first expatriation laws were introduced during the American Civil War in response to the rising numbers of deserters from the Union army. The Nationality Laws of 1940 were a response to growing military concern regarding the approaching war. The amendment of 1944 dealt with the treatment of Japanese purportedly disloyal to war efforts. In the same manner, the Immigration and Nationality Act of 1952 and the Expatriation Act of 1954 were initiated in reaction to fears arising from the Cold War. Hence, I argue that revocation of citizenship is not a random policy that is introduced for election purposes but is contingent upon military conflicts. This is not to say that every military conflict gives rise to debates and policies relating to revocation of citizenship—there are exceptions, as noted below. But when such debates and shifts in policy do arise, they tend to be associated with military conflicts. Citizenship as a social construction has more to do with the practical

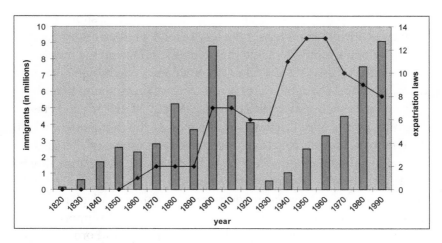

Figure 3.2. Immigration and Provisions of Expatriation. Source of immigration data: Department of Homeland Security, Office of Immigration Statistics, *2003 Yearbook of Immigration Statistics* (September 2004).

needs of the state than with a general, coherent, and stable ideological perception. The boundary disputes around expatriation law in relation to the latest enemy serve both to affirm the national world order of singular national allegiances and to be a vehicle for more transient or contingent issues in the life of the nation.

As the empirical data suggests, the response to the threat to the American polity during the period covered was not necessarily republican. In congressional debates on expatriation during times of war, all three traditions of citizenship were invoked simultaneously. While some of the reaction is clearly an attempt to enlist patriotic or nationalistic sentiments, ethnic and liberal reactions to war were also introduced. Armed conflict is associated with the emergence of revocation laws, but we cannot predict how the enemy is envisaged. At times the opponent is set apart on ethnic grounds (such as the Japanese Americans during the Second World War). In other cases the opponent is defined in republican terms (such as deserters or Americans serving the army of another state). Moreover, every so often, the adversaries are those who defy the economic structure of the United States (such as Communists[28]). The evidence complements two insights suggested by Carl Schmitt.[29] First, even in democratic states the rules apply discriminatory policies through a "state of exception," which verifies their sovereignty and allows for governing outside the boundary of the law. Second, politicians use times of war as an opportunity to define the polity itself. During the debates on the 1940 Nationality Act, the notion of emergency was brought up many times. "Political thought and political instinct prove themselves theoretically and practically in the ability to distinguish friends and enemy. The high points of politics are simultaneously the moments in which the enemy is, in concrete clarity, recognized as the enemy."[30] It appears that politicians are constantly trying to define American nationality by identifying the ultimate adversary. A singular national allegiance can be defined more sharply by an enemy, internal or foreign. Allegiance to the nation is secured in an ongoing state of emergency that supports governance itself. At this level of generality the national world order appears subservient to the need to govern; nationalism is a means.

War is not the only factor that causes variation in expatriation policy. In 1906 it was decided to take away citizenship from naturalized citizens who had acquired this status illegally or by fraud. The next year Congress added several other grounds for expatriation for native-born citizens as well. These statutes were not connected to any threat of war against the United States. Surprisingly, during the First World War, Congress did not enact any new bills regarding the expatriation of citizens. Although armed conflicts have resurfaced, Congress has not legislated any new grounds for taking away American citizenship since 1954. On the contrary, during the Vietnam War several of the existing grounds for expatriation were overturned by the Supreme Court and repealed by Congress.

The conception of citizenship as an overarching and coherent principle of a country has been adopted by most scholars who specialize in citizenship and even more so in the general social scientific literature. This chapter shows that this perception is not present in congressional debates regarding the revocation of citizenship or the legislation of such bills. This disparity reinforces Bourdieu's argument against uncritically adopting categories of practice as categories of analysis. In our present discourse, citizenship is both a practical term that laymen use to describe a person's national affiliation and an analytical concept that describes the relationship between the individual and the state. While the common understanding of citizenship presents it as a coherent worldview, scholars should not assume that it is necessarily so. In accordance with Brubaker who was assessing nationalism, we should not make the practical conception of citizenship central to the theory of citizenship. We are liable to be confused by the force in reality (reification) of the practical conception of citizenship policy that can overwhelm the knowledge established in theory. "Reification is a social process, not only an intellectual practice."[31]

The practice of expatriation, which is clearly an act of regulating unitary national loyalty in the construction of a governable body, can also be contingent on particular political or practical circumstances. In the United States, expatriation was usually initiated during military conflicts, and did not reflect any coherent American ideal, but answered a specific need to regulate a part of the population (deserters, women, Communists, immigrants, or other minorities). However, the policy of expatriation should not be seen only as an internal regulatory practice, but as one that is always connected to at least two states. In other words, it should be seen in the context of international relations.

4

International Relations

It is the general interest of the international community to secure that all its members should recognize that every person should have a nationality and should have one nationality only.
—League of Nations, April 13, 1930

The policy of expatriation was influenced and sometimes dictated by the international relations between the United States and both its allies and its enemies. This chapter follows those considerations by looking at the treaties the United States signed regarding expatriation. From the American Civil War until the Second World War, the United States signed numerous bilateral treaties to ensure the mutual recognition of naturalization. During the First World War, the Allied states that permitted military service in another country without its being considered as transferring allegiance made agreements with one another. In the interwar years, the issue of naturalization resurfaced specifically in relation to the obligation of military service. Therefore, the United States exchanged letters with twenty other countries to make sure American citizens who were also citizens of those countries would not be drafted to their armies during temporary visits. In 1930, the League of Nations hosted a conference that specifically dealt with the then-anomalous condition of dual citizenship. During the Second World War, the United States signed agreements that were similar to those in the First World War and facilitated military service in another country's military without those serving being considered deserters. In all of those interactions between the United States and other counties, there was a constant understanding that dual citizenship should be avoided (except in particular circumstances). Forced expatriation was considered a legitimate state practice to combat multiple national allegiances. After the Second World War, countries around the world began to realize that dual citizenship was not as great a threat as statelessness, and the United Nations organized a conference on this matter. However, even in this convention, forced expatriation was still considered legitimate, as long as it did not cause a person to become stateless. I have found that while some of the expatriation policies were constructed in response to the ideology of exclusive national allegiance, others were practically overturned as responses to states' immediate needs in the international arena (mainly in respect to military efforts).

The Bancroft Treaties

From 1868 to 1937, the same period when most expatriation laws were legislated, the United States entered into twenty-five treaties in regard to nationality transformation. These treaties are known as the Bancroft treaties (Table 5.1),[1] named after the historian and diplomat George Bancroft (1800–1891) who negotiated the first of these agreements with Prussia (officially called the North German Confederation).[2] The goal of these treaties was to regulate the citizenship of those persons who emigrate from one country to another. Dual citizenship was construed as an undesirable outcome, and the treaties were intended to make sure that nationality was acquired in one country at the expense of the other.[3] For Bancroft, double allegiance was to be rejected in the same manner as polygamy.[4]

Most of the Bancroft treaties were formulated in a similar manner. Three of the sections have substantive consequences for the idea of citizenship. The first provision recognized the right of each country's nationals to become naturalized in one of the others. This voluntary expatriation would be officially acknowledged by the home country not after the declaration of intent or the immediate naturalization of the citizen, but after a predetermined period of residence in the host country— usually five years. The second provision maintained that this voluntary expatriation would not remove liability for the trial or punishment of crimes committed in the original country before immigration.

The provision that is most relevant to forced expatriation is related to dual nationality. The two signatories agreed that their nationals who immigrated and became naturalized in the other country and then returned to their original country with the intent not to return where they has been naturalized would be held to have renounced their second citizenship. In other words, naturalized citizens were to lose their citizenship upon return to their former country if they did not intend to remain Americans. Intent was established by showing that the person naturalized in the United States resided for more than two years in his or her former country.

The Bancroft treaties represent the effort of the United States to secure the recognition of voluntary transfer of citizenship; they did not have any problem with the practice of forced expatriation for naturalized citizens who returned to their former country. In 1964 the Supreme Court in *Schneider v. Rusk* invalidated the provision that stripped the citizenship of any naturalized American after three years' continuous residence in his country of origin. Writing for the majority, Justice Douglas stated that "Living abroad, whether the citizen be naturalized or native born, is no badge of lack of allegiance and in no way evidences a voluntary renunciation of nationality and allegiance."[5] However, the Bancroft treaties, which were still in force, contradicted this point of view and should have been abrogated.[6] In 1980, during the administration of President Jimmy Carter, the Bancroft treaties were terminated (with the exception of the treaties with Albania, Bulgaria, and Czechoslovakia).

One of the main reasons that the United States negotiated the Bancroft treaties was connected to the originating ideals and practical concerns of an independent United States citizenship. As mentioned in Chapter 2, the independence of the United States formalized a novel approach regarding the relationship between citizenship and bloodline. Namely, in addition to biological circumstances (birth, marriage, adoption), a person could become an American citizen by naturalization. This new idea was not generally held in other countries in the world where citizenship was treated as being perpetual and could not be easily terminated. Thus, the Bancroft treaties were diplomatic measures aimed at ensuring that foreign citizens could be released from their former citizenship in order to become Americans. On a larger scale, this aim is connected to the problem of dual citizenship. By permitting naturalization (and its termination once the immigrant returns to his or her home country), the countries agree that citizenship can be transferred. However, the Bancroft treaties also maintained that citizenship must be exclusive.

Table 4.1. Bancroft Treaties

Country	Date signed	Year Terminated	Termination
North German Confederation (Prussia)	February 22, 1868	1917	Never revived after First World War
Bavaria	May 26, 1868	1871	Proclamation of the German Empire
Mexico	July 4, 1868		Terminated by Mexico
Baden	July 19, 1868	1871	Proclamation of the German Empire
Württemberg	July 27,1868	1871	Proclamation of the German Empire
Hesse	August 1, 1868	1871	Proclamation of the German Empire
Belgium	November 16, 1868		Terminated by President Jimmy Carter
Sweden and Norway	May 26, 1869	1980	Terminated by President Jimmy Carter
Austro-Hungarian Empire	September 20, 1870	1917	Never revived after First World War
Great Britain	February 23, 1871		Terminated by Great Britain
Denmark	July 20, 1872	1980	Terminated by President Jimmy Carter
Haiti	March 22, 1902	1980	Terminated by President Jimmy Carter
Inter-American Convention	August 13, 1906		Several countries left the treaty
Salvador	March 14, 1908	1980	Terminated by President Jimmy Carter
Brazil	April 27, 1908		Terminated by Brazil
Uruguay	August 10, 1908	1980	Terminated by President Jimmy Carter
Portugal	May 7, 1908	1980	Terminated by President Jimmy Carter
Honduras	June 23, 1908	1980	Terminated by President Jimmy Carter
Peru	October 15, 1907	1980	Terminated by President Jimmy Carter
Nicaragua	December 7, 1908	1980	Terminated by President Jimmy Carter
Costa Rica	June 10, 1911	1980	Terminated by President Jimmy Carter
Bulgaria	November 23, 1923		Never terminated
Czechoslovakia	July 16, 1928	1997	Termination delayed
Albania	April 5, 1932	1991	Termination delayed by the Cold War
Lithuania	October 18, 1937	1980	Terminated by President Jimmy Carter

During the First World War, the United States and other Allied (Entente) powers wanted to make sure that immigration would not impair the war effort in regard to conscription. It was desirable that citizens of the United States in foreign countries and subjects of other Allied countries in the United States would either return to their own country to perform military service in its army or would serve in the army of the country in which they resided. Those citizens who served in a counterpart military would not be liable for military service in the other country and would not be considered deserters in either army. Initially, the United States signed such agreements at the beginning of 1918 with Great Britain and its dominions overseas, and concluded a separate treaty with Canada. At the request of President Woodrow Wilson, the conventions were redrafted by mutual consent. Four months later a treaty was signed again with Great Britain and Canada. The agreements ignited confusion regarding the age requirements for military service. Were Americans in Great Britain subject to the local age of conscription or to the American Draft Act of 1917?[7] The issue was resolved by an exchange of letters between the British embassy in Washington and Robert Lansing, the secretary of state of the United States. It was agreed that, although it was not specified in the original treaty, the age of military obligation for Americans in Great Britain would be determined by the Draft Act of 1917. Later on in 1918, the United States signed similar treaties with France, Italy, and Greece.[8] All of the agreements became obsolete at the end of the First World War.

These treaties had significant implications for the revocation of citizenship. By law, the United States revoked American citizenship for desertion[9] from 1865 until this provision was declared unconstitutional by the Supreme Court in *Trop v. Dulles* (1958) and finally was repealed by the Congress in 1978. During the First World War, men aged twenty-one to thirty were required to register for military service. Thus, unless those treaties had been signed, a citizen who served in the armed forces of another Allied country would have been treated as changing his national allegiance and would therefore lose his citizenship. In the conscription treaty with Great Britain, it was explicitly stated that "[no] citizen or subject of either country who, under the provisions of this Convention, enters the military service of the other, shall, by reason of such service, be considered, after this Convention shall have expired or after his discharge, to have lost his nationality or to be under any allegiance to His Britannic Majesty or to the United States as the case may be."[10]

With the conclusion of the First World War, the nineteenth-century problem in which foreign powers required conscription of their nationals after naturalization in the United States (see Chapter 2) returned to the diplomatic table. The Department of State was daily required to consider cases in which persons born in the United States or of foreign parentage and naturalized as American citizens were impressed into the military service of the countries of their parents' nationality or their former citizenship. It was estimated that between three and four thousand such cases were brought to the attention of the Department of State— over half in Italy, but also in Poland, Czechoslovakia, Greece, Portugal, France, Turkey, and Yugoslavia. The ideal was to eliminate dual citizenship. In 1928, Frank B. Kellogg,[11] the secretary of state, in a letter to Stephen Porter, the chairman of the Committee on Foreign Affairs of the House of Representatives, wrote that "It is believed that the desideratum in this matter would be the conclusion of international agreements, supplemented by such legislation as might be necessary, under which the anomalous condition of dual nationality would be definitely terminated."[12] In the same letter Kellogg acknowledged that many Americans currently held dual citizenship, but for him the pressing matter concerned American citizens who temporarily visited the county of their second nationality and could be forced into military service in the second country. Therefore, a joint resolution of Congress was introduced to begin negotiations for international agreements that would protect naturalized citizens (after more than five years) who visited their former country (for less than a year) from being conscripted into military service in that country.[13]

During 1929, the secretary of state and his staff exchanged letters with diplomats and ministers in Belgium, France, Estonia, Bulgaria, Denmark, Estonia, Latvia, Lithuania, Finland, Great Britain, Greece, Italy, the Netherlands, Norway, Poland, Portugal, Romania, Spain, Sweden, and Yugoslavia to clarify issues relating to their citizens who had been naturalized in the United States.[14] Specifically, the United States wanted to make sure that naturalized American citizens would pay taxes, be drafted to the army, or be punished for not doing the former after the date of their naturalization. Therefore, the Bancroft treaties that were signed after these deliberations (with Bulgaria in 1923, Albania in 1932, and Lithuania in 1937) included provisions that dealt with military service. All three treaties stated that "Nationals of either country, who have or shall become naturalized in the territory of the other country shall not, upon returning to the country of former nationality for a temporary stay, be required to perform military service or any other act of allegiance, or punished for the original act of emigration, or for the failure to respond to a call for military service, liability for which did not accrue until after bona fide residence was acquired in the territory of the country whose nationality was obtained by naturalization."[15] Hence, in this provision, while dual citizenship might was acknowledged to be a reality, the idea that allegiance should not be divided was affirmed. Upon naturalization, the naturalized citizens should not undertake (or be forced to undertake) any acts of loyalty to their former country.

In the 1930s, in addition to the Bancroft treaties, the United States was engaged in two international efforts to reduce the unwanted condition of dual citizenship. On the one hand, the United States signed bilateral treaties with Norway (1930), Sweden (1933), Switzerland (1937), and Finland (1939) regarding the military service of persons with dual nationality. Unlike the Bancroft treaties, the military service treaties did not emphasize the mutual acceptance of naturalization, but dealt exclusively with military service and other acts of allegiance for persons with dual nationality. For this reason, I have included the treaty with Lithuania, which dealt both with the issue of naturalization and military service, as a Bancroft treaty. On the other hand, the United States participated in the League of Nations' Convention on Certain Questions Relating to the Conflict of Nationality Laws, also called the Hague Conference of 1930.[16]

The Hague Conference of 1930

Until the Second World War, it was still believed that it was desirable for the national ideal to be protected. Dual citizenship was perceived as an imminent threat to the continuation of this world order that supposes a one-on-one relationship between the individual and the state. In this setting voluntary renunciation was encouraged and forced expatriation was recommended to regulate the inconsistencies that were produced through immigration or border shifts. The opposition to dual citizenship became internationally institutionalized with the 1930 League of Nations' Convention on Certain Questions Relating to the Conflict of Nationality Laws, which entered into force on July 1, 1937. The convention explicitly stated that "it is the general interest of the international community to secure that all its members should recognize that every person should have a nationality and *should have one nationality only*." Therefore, "the ideal towards which the efforts of humanity should be directed in this domain is the abolition of all cases both of statelessness and of double nationality."[17] Accordingly, protection of dual citizens is limited to one country only (Articles 4 and 5), and renunciation must be authorized by all countries (Article 6). The gravity of the proposition is indicated by appealing to an "ideal" that "humanity" should strive for. Chapter III of the convention dealt specifically with the nationality of married women. Although the loss of nationality for marrying foreigners was not prohibited, the signatories wanted to make sure that this common practice would not cause dual citizenship or statelessness. For example, the naturalization of the husband during marriage would not automatically change the nationality of the wife, and a woman's loss of nationality as a consequence of her marriage would be conditioned upon her acquiring a new nationality. The convention failed to provide for a woman's citizenship independent of her husband's, nor did it state that citizenship should not be revoked automatically upon marriage to a foreigner, and, for this reason, the United States did not sign the convention.[18]

The Convention on Certain Questions Relating to the Conflict of Nationality Laws was the product of a larger conference entitled the First Conference for the Codification of International Law, which that met in The Hague.[19] The conference marked the launching of a new effort for the advancement of international law, but produced meager results in that respect. While the particular needs and interests of each of the countries prevented the delegates from achieving working instruments of codified international law, the conference did signify an honorable first attempt at that goal. It was composed of both members and non-members of the League of Nations, and its agenda had three issues: nationality, territorial waters, and the responsibilities of states. Only the first dealt with expatriation and dual nationality and produced the above-mentioned convention, a protocol relating to military obligations in certain cases of double nationality, and two protocols concerning statelessness. Although the convention relating to dual citizenship was agreed upon and formulated according to the ideal that humanity should combat dual nationality, the delegates did not agree on the steps that should facilitate this principle. The Hague convention relied on the unofficial Harvard Draft Code written by the faculty of Harvard's Law School. The Harvard Draft Code was more innovative than the conclusions of the conference itself, as governments were hesitant to place constraints on the rights of states to legislate on matters of nationality.[20] For example, the Harvard Draft did not include any articles on denaturalization while the conference's Article 7 explicitly permits states to expatriate their citizens.

The protocol on the military obligations of dual nationals was similar to the bilateral agreements reached previously by the United States during the First World War. It provided that persons habitually residing in one country, and closely connected with that country, shall be exempted from military obligations in any other country of which they are also nationals. However, it also states that such exemption may entail the loss of the nationality of the country in which it is enjoyed. In other words, there is no acceptance of dual nationality, and although allegiance can be transferred, it is exclusive. Unlike the Convention on Certain Questions Relating to the Conflict of Nationality Laws, the Protocol Relating to Military Obligations in Certain Cases of Double Nationality was signed and ratified by the United States on August 3, 1932. The two protocols on statelessness dealt with relatively infrequent problems of persons born to a father with no, or unknown, nationality; and permanently indigent or criminal persons who are left stateless because of the revocation of their citizenship under the responsibility of another state.

While the interwar years brought to the fore the concern of forced conscription to another army, the Second World War revived the concerns that had arisen during the First World War that individuals who served in a the military of an Allied country would be punished for desertion, for departing the United States to avoid military service, or for serving in another army—acts that might lead to the loss of American citizenship according to the Nationality Act of 1940. Therefore, the United States exchanged notes with Canada (1942), Poland (1942), Yugoslavia (1942), Australia (1942), Belgium (1942), Cuba (1942), Norway (1943), Czechoslovakia (1943), Brazil (1943), Ecuador (1945), and France

(1948) regarding the military service of foreign nationals residing in the United States (and vice versa). With the exception of the exchange with France, in which discussion was retroactive, all the other agreements specifically recognized the joint war effort and therefore were meant to enable the conscription of individuals to the army of the other Allied country. For example, the letter to the Australian minister stated that "This government recognizes that from the standpoint of morale of the individuals concerned and the over-all military effort of the countries at war with the Axis Powers, it would be desirable to permit certain classes of individuals who have registered or who may register under the Selective Training and Service Act of 1940, as amended, to enlist in the armed forces of a co-belligerent country, should they desire to do so."[21] These deliberations did not discuss the issue of dual citizenship per se, as many countries including the United States drafted non-citizens to their military. However, these agreements did implicitly address one of the implications of serving in another country's army—that of losing American citizenship. After the war, on March 31, 1947, these agreements were terminated upon the termination of functions of the United States Selective Service System.[22]

The exchange of notes with Paris (1948) concerned persons who were nationals of both countries (the United States and France) and encountered difficulties as a result of their military obligations in the two countries. The French minister of foreign affairs and the United States ambassador to Paris agreed that serving the military during the war of 1939–1945 in either country would fulfill the military obligation of both nations. In essence, the United States, in contradiction to its official policy, acknowledged and approved the existence of dual citizenship. However, this tolerance was temporary and was related to particular circumstances. Many years would pass before the State Department would explicitly announce that acquiring another citizenship or serving in the army of another country did not indicate the intent to relinquish American citizenship and would not cause the loss of such citizenship.

The Shift in International Law

It was the horrible consequences of the Second World War and the Holocaust that made the international community aware that it is not the lack of protection for states that threatens the world, but lack of protection for people. Recognizing this, the international community passed a resolution regarding the loss of citizenship in the United Nations Convention on the Reduction of Statelessness in 1961.[23] The convention, which entered into force in 1975, was based on the previous 1954 U.N. convention that determined the status of stateless persons. In order to eradicate statelessness, the convention held that "A Contracting State shall not deprive a person of his nationality if such deprivation would render him stateless" and that "If the law of a Contracting State entails loss or renunciation of nationality, such renunciation shall not result in loss of nationality unless the person concerned possesses or acquires another nationality."[24] The convention does not go so far as to pledge states to offer citizenship to persons whom dire circumstances leave without membership in a polity. Nevertheless, statelessness, rather than "statefulness," was perceived as the threat to humanity.[25] Again, this transformation occurred not as a result of non-national ideology but as an imperative measure to protect the millions of refugees and stateless people who emerged from war and forced into migration.

While the United Nations agreed that statelessness should be avoided and placed binding measures on states with that goal in mind, forced expatriation was not prohibited. Article 8, which deals with forced expatriation, maintains that a contracting state can retain the right to deprive a citizen of his or her nationality if the citizen's actions are inconsistent with his or her duty of loyalty to the contracting state. Such disloyalties occur when a person (1) has, in disregard of an express prohibition by the contracting state, rendered or continued to render services to, or received or continued to receive emoluments from, another state; (2) has conducted him- or herself in a manner seriously prejudicial to the vital interests of the state; or (3) has taken an oath, or made a formal declaration, of allegiance to another state, or given definite evidence of his or her determination to repudiate allegiance to the contracting state. Nevertheless, forced expatriation is prohibited if the citizen does not possess another citizenship. Article 5 deals with the loss of citizenship as the consequence of any change in the personal status of a person, such as marriage, termination of marriage, and adoption. Article 6 deals with the loss of citizenship in the case that the spouse or parents have lost their citizenship. In both cases, the forced expatriation of a person or of his or her spouse or parents is allowed, as long as it is written in the laws of the state and providing that loss of nationality does not leave the expatriated person stateless.

Although not directly influencing the international relations of the United States, the Council of Europe, an international organization that is composed today of forty-seven countries in Europe (not only the members of the European Union), passed several treaties that can illuminate the attitude of the Western world to dual citizenship and forced expatriation.

The first convention was drafted in 1963. At that time, European countries held the traditional national perspective that dual nationality was a threat to the stability of Europe. Since "the aim of the Council of Europe is to achieve a greater unity between its Members," and "cases of multiple nationality are liable to cause difficulties," the member states should jointly "reduce as far as possible the number of cases of multiple nationality."[26] The 1963 Convention on the Reduction of Cases of Multiple Nationality and Military Obligations in Cases of Multiple Nationality concluded that nationals of the contracting states would lose their former nationality if they were of full age and acquired, of their own free will, the nationality of another contracting state. It was clearly stated that renunciations should not be prohibited (to minimize dual citizenship). As in most other treaties relating to dual nationality, one of the main goals was to regulate the military obligation of dual citizens. In the 1963 convention it was decided that dual citizens would be required to fulfill their military obligation in relation to only one of the states whose citizenship they held.[27] Both in Schmitt's dictum about having an enemy as an opportunity to define the polity itself and in the association of military obligations with national belonging, a defining linkage between war and the national world order is apparent.

Three additional protocols were added as amendments to the 1963 convention. In 1977 two protocols were added[28] to regulate the systematic transfer of information regarding the acquisition of a second citizenship within the member states and to reduce the residence obstacles for renunciation. Neither of those amendments questions the validity of the assumption that dual citizenship as a condition should be avoided. However, a third protocol in 1993[29] did maintain that the strict principle of exclusive nationality should be relaxed (but not abandoned). Therefore, the treaty allowed for three additional cases of dual nationality for second-generation migrants, for spouses of mixed marriages, and for their children.

The main breakthrough came only in 1997. In that year the Council of Europe negotiated another international treaty regarding dual national-ity.[30] In contrast to the 1963 Convention on the Reduction of Cases of Multiple Nationality, this new agreement privileges individual over state interest and thus sees dual nationality as an acceptable phenomenon.[31] Spiro claims that this treaty "may mark a watershed in global percep-tions of the status [of dual citizenship], which in turn could point to some acceptance of the status [of dual citizenship] as a matter of right rather than grace."[32] However, this transformation was not accompanied by an equivalent change regarding the revocation of citizenship.

Although the treaty does maintain that citizenship should not be re-voked arbitrarily, cannot be associated with marriage (or the dissolution of marriage), and cannot make the person stateless, forced expatriation is permitted and viewed as a legitimate act on the part of a state. Article 7 specifies the instances where forced deprivation of nationality is lawful, including voluntary acquisition of another nationality, voluntary service in a foreign military force, serious prejudicial acts against the interests of the state, and even lack of a genuine link between citizens who reside abroad and their home country. This section suggests that although dual citizenship is accepted, it has yet to be publicly embraced or universally perceived as a positive status. Even the 1997 European Convention on Nationality did not completely dispense with the ideal that while dual citizenship might be an unavoidable condition (stemming from the con-flicting citizenship regimes in different countries), it is not acceptable to publicly and explicitly acquire the nationality of another state.

Scholars have debated the reasons for the United States' taking such a negative view of dual citizenship and instituting the policy of forced expatriation. The most common justification is related to the incompre-hensibility of the idea of dual citizenship for much of its history, which was likened to political bigamy.[33] Peter Spiro has argued that the need for an international regulatory mechanism that eradicates dual national-ity is connected to issues of diplomatic protection.[34] Another difficulty was the need to regulate military service and other acts that suppos-edly require undivided allegiance. These considerations should be seen as part of a whole and not viewed separately. Practical needs of state (such as issuing protection to citizens abroad or ensuring the loyalty of the army) are always intimately linked with the dominant perceptions of citizenship at that particular moment (i.e. that national allegiance cannot be divided or multiple). In addition, policies are rooted in the hegemonic cultural perception of the time. Thus, while considering actual cases of dual citizenship, the consular and diplomatic officers of the United States abroad also included assumptions regarding gender, religion, capitalism, and race.

5

Consular Dilemmas

The protection of the flag is intended for those who intend
to dwell under it.
—Congressman James Perkins, 1907

Since independence, American diplomatic and consular officers
around the world were constantly deliberating about practical issues
relating to the transfer of allegiance. From the point of view of official
representatives of the United States abroad, it was essential to determine
with absolute certainty the final allegiance of each and every American
outside the United States, and to proffer uniformity of treatment for
them all. Additionally, the officers had to make sure that no one who
had effectually expatriated him- or herself from the United States
would receive the protection conferred upon American citizens. At the
same time, it was crucial that no loyal American would be denied such
protection. To these ends, the Department of State sent out detailed
instructions for determining national allegiance. At times, those
instructions came in the form of answers to consular dilemmas arising
from a particular case; at other times, such clarifications came in the
form of circulars addressing a general principle regarding American
nationals abroad.

The Protection of Americans Abroad

As mentioned in Chapter 3, the idea of forced expatriation was legislated
in 1865 to address army deserters. It was only in 1907 that the United
States specified additional expatriating acts. However, even beforehand,
the State Department was pondering the question of when a citizen
forfeits his or her rights as a citizen, and especially the right to protection while abroad. According to international law, states have complete
territorial sovereignty. Therefore, an American citizen abroad is under

the jurisdiction of the foreign government and its laws. Since the nineteenth century, however, it has also been understood that a person who is abroad is entitled to the protection of his or her own government in cases where prejudice is clearly evident. For instance, in 1851 Daniel Webster, the American secretary of state, argued that "It is undoubtedly true that an American citizen who goes into a foreign country, although he owes local and temporary allegiance to that country, is yet, if he performs no other act changing his condition, entitled to the protection of his own government; and if, without violation of any municipal law, he should be treated unjustly, he would have a right to claim that protection; and the interposition of the American Government in his favor would be considered as a justifiable interposition."[1] The negative attitude toward dual citizenship was probably related to the same concern that extending diplomatic protection to such citizens might result in a conflict between the nations.[2]

During the nineteenth century, it was customary that in some instances governments ought not to intervene in regard to the treatment of their citizens outside their territory. However, there were no laws that explicitly articulated those instances in which the United States should withhold protection for Americans abroad. Therefore, representatives of the United States abroad had to interpret the general principles of expatriation. For example, if an American had settled in another country, it was understood that he or she had ceased to be an American citizen and thus did not have the right to demand the protection of the U.S. government. Since there was no way to categorically establish whether a person intended to stay abroad temporarily or had moved with the purpose of remaining there, the State Department had to rely on additional indicators. These included "letters of domiciliation," swearing allegiance to another political entity, voluntarily withdrawing property from the United States, failing to pay taxes in the United States, and going into public service in another country, as well as other indications that imply permanent residence in a foreign country, evasion of the duties of citizenship in the United States, and of course, open renunciation. While the government claimed not to discriminate between native-born and naturalized citizens in according them protection while they were abroad, this distinction did have great importance in determining whether an American had expatriated him- or herself. Secretary of State John Hay wrote in 1899 that "a naturalized citizen who returns to the country of his origins and there resides without any tangible manifestation of an intention to return to the United States may therefore generally be assumed to have lost the right to receive the protection of the United States." [3] In the mid-nineteenth century, it was agreed that it was the responsibility of the citizen to prove that residence abroad was temporary and that or she he intended to return to the United States.

The policy of the State Department forbade the granting of diplomatic protection to citizens who permanently resided in a foreign country. Again, this served to prevent a situation akin to dual citizenship. However, the State Department was willing in some cases to accept that American citizens who resided abroad for prolonged periods of time could continue to be American citizens when health or business reasons existed for their doing so.

Thus, for example, Thomas F. Bayard, who served as secretary of state between 1885 and 1889, argued in a letter sent in 1887 that "citizens of the United States who go abroad for reasons of health, and remain abroad many years hoping to come back, yet are prevented from doing so by continuing illness"[4] should have American diplomatic protection. By way of example, Bayard referred to an American woman who had been residing in the south of France for more than twenty years but had not lost her entitlement for protection or her property rights in New York for this reason. Similar arguments were given in the case of William Strablheim, a native-born American living in Switzerland. The State Department agreed to renew his passport in 1902, despite his residence abroad, as his physical condition prevented him from returning to the United States.

Another circumstance in which American citizens would retain government protection was when their residence abroad was a result of conducting commercial enterprise as an agent of American business. In the abovementioned letter, Bayard concluded that "The continued presence of such agents at their scene is essential to the maintenance of some of our great industries . . . [and thus, they are] entitled to the protection of the Department, no matter how long they remain away."[5] Here, it is perfectly clear that national or public or commercial interest was the guiding consideration, rather than concern for the individual. Whether provisions to make the national order flexible have the effect of undercutting and pointing beyond it or are merely necessary maintenance measures is not always clear. Moreover, the mercantilist perspective was even employed with regard to naturalized citizens who came from foreign lands because their familiarity with the language and traditions of such lands was likely to better enhance commerce. John Hay reaffirmed this principle in a circular in 1899 by arguing that "the most favorable of all [circumstances for remaining American] is that the applicant is residing abroad in representation and extension of legitimate American enterprises."[6]

A third distinction (in contrast to a later understanding of intent) is connected to the perceptions of the Orient that were dominant in the West.[7] In 1887, the State Department dealt with the case of several individuals living in Turkey. They were second- generation descendants of Americans born abroad, whose father had never resided in the United States. Since the United States does not subscribe to the *jus sanguinis* principle, citizenship is not passed on according to bloodline; so those men should not have been considered Americans. However, it was argued that due to their residence in a Mohammedan (Muslim) country rather than a Christian one, they were not only exempt from the jurisdiction of the Turkish tribunals but were entitled to the protection of the United States as American citizens. In other words, the United States agreed to grant inherited citizenship (contrary to its own principles) on the grounds of extraterritoriality. As long as the Americans resided in distinctive American communities, they would not lose their domicile or citizenship in the United States—no matter how long they remained in Turkey. In a later communication, it was argued that the policy extended to Americans living in an extraterritorial jurisdiction of the United States also applied to residents in a semi-barbarous country. Except in the case of naturalized citizens who were previously subjects of such countries, Americans could indefinitely prolong their residence in such countries, "since obviously they cannot become subjects of the native government without grave peril to their safety."[8]

Explaining Expatriation Policy

Owing to the discomfort of the consular and diplomatic officers who did not have a concrete set of rules regarding the protection of Americans living abroad, Congress decided to legislate the 1907 Expatriation Act (described in Chapter 3). Section 3, which dealt with expatriation, was deemed the most important part of the bill: "We all desire that the full protection of the United States should be extended everywhere and at all times over every man who is a bona fide citizen of this land; but the protection of the flag is intended for those who intend to dwell under it. It should not be perverted to a fraudulent shield under which those who do not intend to share our lot seek to escape from the responsibilities they may be under to other governments."[9] The 1907 Expatriation Act listed the grounds for an American to lose his or her citizenship but American representatives abroad still faced dilemmas regarding specific cases. Some of those concerns were resolved and explicated in the instructions that came from Washington.

Immediately after the 1907 Expatriation Act was passed in Congress, the State Department disseminated a circular to explain this new law. As mentioned before, as a result of the new act, a naturalized citizen would expatriate him or herself after residing for two years in the country of his or her origin, or five years in any other country. This presumption could be overcome in three cases: (1) if residence abroad was principally related to American trade and commerce; (2) if residence abroad was in good faith for reasons of health or education; (3) if there was some unforeseen and controlling exigency that prevented the person from carrying out the intention to return to the United States. A separate communication was sent to explain the expatriation of women who married foreigners.

In a 1908 circular, the Department of State discussed the protection of Americans in China in light of the 1907 Expatriation Act. Although at the time the United States prohibited immigration from China[10] the memorandum did give an example of a naturalized Chinese citizen. It described a situation in which a person of Chinese origin who had acquired Hawaiian citizenship during Hawaiian independence and became naturalized as an American citizen upon the annexation of Hawaii (1894). The circular asserted that if this Chinese American were to return to China and reside there for more than two years, he would be presumed to have ceased to be an American citizen; non-Chinese naturalized Americans would lose their citizenship after five years of residence in China.

In addition to the sections that dealt with American trade and commerce and an unforeseen and controlling exigency, it was argued that even regular employment that was not inconsistent with American interest could override the presumption that citizenship should be revoked. This was even true if the employment was with the Chinese government, as long as the citizen intended to return to the United States. Another exception to the residence requirement of naturalized citizens was made if the citizen was a regularly appointed missionary of a recognized American church organization. There was a link between a notion of legitimate government and Christianity in state policy.

A circular disseminated in 1911 added another exception to the 1907 Expatriation Act. A naturalized citizen could overcome the presumption of expatriation by showing that he or she had made definite arrangements to return immediately to the United States for permanent residence. Such preparations included the disposition of property and effects, arrangements in regard to passage of the rest of the family, and "whenever practicable, the exhibition of the applicant's steamship ticket."[11] Although the perception that national identity should be exclusive was clearly expressed in the 1907 Expatriation Act, at the beginning of the twentieth century, religious, orientalist, and capitalistic sentiments could supersede the presumptions about relinquishing American citizenship. We will see (in Chapter 7) that by the end of the century, lawyers and administrators on the Board of Appellate Review usually were not able to be lenient regarding the law. Therefore, health, missionary work, or commerce were not legitimate excuses for maintaining American citizenship.

In 1913, another new interpretation was introduced when Washington decided that the 1907 Expatriation Act did not apply to naturalized citizens who resided in countries near the United States. Therefore, American diplomatic and consular officers in Central America, Mexico, Panama, Canada, and the West Indies were instructed that naturalized citizens employed in a legitimate corporation or company owned or controlled by American citizens should continue to be protected by the United States as citizens.

The beginning of the First World War brought additional difficulties in respect to the Expatriation Act of 1907. This act maintained that American citizens would be deemed to have expatriated themselves by naturalization in a foreign state or taking its oath of allegiance. The Department of State received many inquiries from Americans who wanted to enlist in a foreign army but were concerned that they would lose their American citizenship. Although the revocation of citizenship on the grounds of joining another army was introduced only in the Nationality Act of 1940, the reality before that was that the conscripted person would typically need to take an oath of allegiance to the foreign state. Therefore, U.S. citizens were permitted to enlist only in branches of foreign armies that did not require such an oath. Moreover, a memorandum from 1915 stressed that American citizens were obliged to observe the neutrality of the United States in the European conflict and avoid any participation in it. Once the United States joined the war, its interest was in regulating (but not prohibiting) the enlistment of American citizens in Allied countries (see Chapter 4). The state was sensitive to its citizens as its representatives in the international context.

Another difficulty introduced by the war was an increase in the number of applications for the renewal of passports or for recovering United States citizenship. The Department of State was worried that many of the applicants were former American citizens who had abandoned the United States, usually in favor of their native lands, but because of the war wished to seek refuge in the United States. It was suspected that the real reason was not a renewal of American national sentiments, but the desire to avoid payment of war taxes or to evade military service (on the part of the applicants themselves or of their children). Therefore, in 1916 the State Department retracted some of the generous interpretations of the 1907 Expatriation Act that had been granted to former American citizens. One stipulation was that making definite arrangements to settle permanently in the United States would no longer be sufficient to override the presumption for expatriation. Second, the consular and diplomatic outposts would stop issuing temporary American passports for such people. Third, the State Department concluded that the nature of any "unforeseen and controlling exigency" (which previously would have been a legitimate reason for not returning to the United States within a prescribed period of time) would be limited such that failure to accumulate sufficient means to return to the United States because of unsuccessful business affairs, for example, rather than some special misfortune, would not be considered a legitimate excuse for not return-ing to the United States.

Washington kept its representatives abroad informed regarding the changes in expatriation policies. As we will see in the next chapter, during the twentieth century the United States Supreme Court ruled against many of the grounds for forced expatriation. Consequently, Congress repealed many of the sections of the law regarding the revocation of citizenship. This process culminated at the end of the century. In April 1990, all the diplomatic and consular outposts were informed of a new standard whereby citizens who obtained naturalization in a foreign state, made a declaration of allegiance to a foreign state, or accepted a non-policy position in a foreign state were permitted to retain their American citizenship.

6

Supreme Court Rulings

As long as a person does not voluntarily renounce or
abandon his citizenship . . . I believe his fundamental right
of citizenship is secure.
—Chief Justice Earl Warren, 1958

Several decisions made by the Supreme Court have shifted the
benchmark for stripping away citizenship. In the past, the policy of
expatriation was introduced mainly as a punishment for "un-American
activities." Since 1960, the focus has shifted to the citizen's own desire
to be expatriated. That is, citizenship is revoked only after the state
has shown that the citizen intended to relinquish this status of his or
her own volition. During the recent and continuing "War on Terror"
politicians have been once again calling to change the interpretation
of expatriation policy in the Constitution—so far, without success.
In a previous chapter, I covered the initiation of expatriation policies
in the United States. The present chapter looks at the current state of
expatriation, including conflicting political and philosophical ideals that
shape it, legal developments that affect it, and shifting power relations
among the three branches of government, which also have a role.
Different understandings of the purpose and meaning of the national
order and of citizenship can coexist, although they are in conflict within
a single polity.

During the second half of the twentieth century, the balance of power
in decisions regarding to expatriation shifted from Congress and the
administration toward the courts. In 1958, the Supreme Court effectively
declared its ultimate authority over such matters and thus restricted,
for the first time, the power of Congress to forcibly revoke American
citizenship. The Court held that the use of denationalization as a punishment was unconstitutional under the Eighth Amendment since it
constitutes "cruel and unusual punishment." However, the Court was

still divided over the grounds for expatriation. Some justices maintained that only a voluntary renunciation could terminate the tie between the individual and the state; others continued to maintain that this connection should be dependent on the circumstances and that Congress, as the representative of the people, should have the last word. While the Court resolved this quandary in 1967, arguing that involuntary loss of citizenship was prohibited by the Fourteenth Amendment, it took the legislative branch twenty-five additional years to repeal most of the grounds for forced expatriation. It took even longer for the administration to accept that change, and it can be argued that some members of society still assume that some acts deserve to be punished by a revocation of American citizenship.

Today, there are seven remaining acts in the Immigration and Nationality Act Section 349 that could result in the loss of citizenship—except for subsection (a) 5 (renunciation of American nationality in a foreign state), all were originally intended to penalize felonious Americans. Subsections (a) 1 and 2 (becoming naturalized and taking an oath of allegiance in a foreign state) were both legislated in the 1907 Expatriation Act. Although the underlying motive of this legislation was ostensibly to prevent problems associated with the possession of dual nationality or allegiance, the statute clearly authorized the denationalization of U.S. citizens who had no desire to lose their American nationality.[1] Subsections (a) 3 and 4 (serving in the army or employment in the government of a foreign state) were initiated during the Second World War in the Nationality Act of 1940. Although some congressmen explicitly said this was not a punishment, this statute included a penalty for actions that did not involve the assumption of a new nationality. Subsection (a) 6 (renouncing American citizenship in the territory of the United States during war) was clearly established in 1944 to allow the expatriation on racial grounds of Japanese Americans who were held in relocation camps throughout the United States. Subsection (a) 7 (committing any act of treason) was legislated in the 1954 Expatriation Act and refers to the persecution of Communists and their sympathizers during the Cold War. In addition to the implicit punitive goal of this legislation, which is apparent from the deliberations around the passage of this law, this decree explicitly refers to the violation of several sections of Title 18 of the U.S. Code—Crimes and Criminal Procedure. As I mentioned, the only

exception is subsection (a) 5, which deals with the voluntary renunciation of American citizenship but even here, there are many reasons to
suspect that this ground for expatriation is not entirely voluntary.

In the previous chapters, I showed that, starting at the end of the
nineteenth century, treason, desertion, or any act that appeared to imply
the adoption of a new nationality could be a reason to expatriate citizens. Today, those acts must be combined not only with the purpose
of acquiring another nationality, but also with the intent to renounce
American citizenship. More importantly, it is incumbent upon the state
to prove this intent. Thus the main change, beginning in the second
half of the twentieth century, is that, today, the State Department is required to prove that acts implying the adoption of a new nationality
were undertaken with the explicit intention of relinquishing American
citizenship.

The Supreme Court's Interpretation of Expatriation

During the second half of the twentieth century, the perception of
expatriation as a policy changed dramatically. This transformation
can be attributed largely to initiatives of the judicial branch, beginning
with Warren Court. Beginning in 1958, judges started to question the
constitutional legality of forced expatriation. Over the years, the U.S.
Supreme Court has overturned many of the previous grounds for the
revocation of citizenship as unconstitutional. In compliance with the
Court, Congress repealed the provisions that revoked citizenship for
draft evasion, desertion, voting in a foreign country, the 1952 addition
to the subversion principle that allowed the government to deport
immigrants or naturalized citizens engaged in subversive, especially
allegedly communist, activities, and residence abroad. A perusal of the
Court's decisions on these issues makes it patently clear that expatriation
was originally initiated as a punishment. In other words, in concluding
that the loss of citizenship should not be inflicted as a punishment, the
Supreme Court highlighted the fact that in the past it had indeed been
viewed as a penalty.

Private Albert L. Trop was a natural-born citizen of the United
States who deserted from an army stockade in 1944. He was subsequently court-martialed, found guilty, and sentenced to three years of hard

labor, forfeiture of pay, and a dishonorable discharge. In 1952, Trop applied for a passport in New York. His application was denied because the Nationality Act of 1940 provided that members of the armed forces of the United States who deserted would lose their citizenship.[2] Trop filed suit in federal courts seeking declaratory judgment that he was a U.S. citizen. The district court ruled in favor of the government, and the U.S. Court of Appeals for the Second Circuit upheld the decision of the district court.

On the appeal in *Trop v. Dulles*,[3] a five-to-four decision of the Supreme Court concluded that stripping of American citizenship as a punishment was unconstitutional in terms of the Eighth Amendment's prohibition on inflicting "cruel and unusual punishment" on American citizens, and therefore reversed the district court decision. As Chief Justice Earl Warren wrote,

> It is a form of punishment more primitive than torture, for it destroys for the individual the political existence that was centuries in the development. . . . This punishment is offensive to the cardinal principles for which the constitution stands. It subjects the individual to a fate of ever-increasing fear and distress. . . . Citizenship is not a license that expires upon misbehavior. The duties of citizenship are numerous, and the discharge of many of these obligations is essential to the security and wellbeing of the Nation. . . . But citizenship is not lost every time a duty of citizenship is shirked. And the deprivation of citizenship is not a weapon that the government may use to express its displeasure at a citizen's conduct, however reprehensible that conduct may be. As long as a person does not voluntarily renounce or abandon his citizenship . . . I believe his fundamental right of citizenship is secure.[4]

Chief Justice Earl Warren maintained that citizenship should not be rescinded by Congress. This novel interpretation of the power of the United States Congress to strip away citizenship corresponds to the "agenda of rights" promoted by the Warren Court. That is, the commitment of the justices in the 1960s and 1970s was to a tolerant society where people's identities would flourish. During the sixteen years (1953–1969) during which Earl Warren served as Chief Justice, the Courts regularly handed down opinions that transformed American constitutional doctrine and American society.[5] Although the most famous decision was in *Brown v. Board of Education* (1954),[6] wherein the Supreme Court declared that racial segregation in public schools was unconstitutional, the Warren Court made many other transformational rulings, including for example, ensuring political equality in the form of "one person, one vote" by ruling that state congressional districts of unequal size were unconstitutional;[7] the requirement of what has come to be known as the "Miranda warning" in which police must inform arrested persons that they need not answer questions and that they may have an attorney present during questioning;[8] and the recognition of the constitutional right to privacy when the Court struck down a Connecticut statute that prohibited the dissemination of birth control information.[9]

Even today, this line of reasoning involving distancing expatriation from other punitive measures is the predominant approach. Hence, it is not surprising that in *Afroyim v. Rusk* (1967)[10] and, similarly, in *Vance v. Terrazas* (1980),[11] the Court held that Congress lacked the power of involuntary expatriation and that the most the U.S. government could do was to formally recognize an individual's voluntary renunciation of his or her American citizenship. However, while the language of the law has tried to reclassify revocation of citizenship as non-punitive, this procedure was originally intimately connected to various punitive measures— specifically, for transferring one's national loyalty. [12]

Beys Afroyim was born in 1893 in Ryki, Poland, as Ephraim Bernstein. He emigrated to the United States when he was nineteen and became a naturalized citizen in 1926. As a painter and sculptor in New York City, he was director and teacher at the Afroyim Experimental Art School from 1927 to 1946. Subsequently, Beys Afroyim's activities within the Communist Party of America led him and his wife, Soshana Afroyim, to leave the United States and spend some months in Cuba. In Havana, Soshana, an artist of the Modernist period, had her first exhibition in 1948 in the *Circulo de Bellas Artes*. During the McCarthy era, when it became unsafe for the couple to live in the United States, they left for Europe and eventually arrived in Israel in 1950.

Being Jewish, Afroyim was automatically granted Israeli citizenship under the Law of Return. He voluntarily voted in the Israeli election in 1951. In 1960, Afroyim tried to renew his U.S. passport, but the State Department denied his application. The State Department argued that according to Section 401(e) of the Nationality Act of 1940, a United States citizen loses his or her citizenship if he or she votes in a political election

in a foreign state. Afroyim sued Dean Rusk in his official capacity as secretary of state and head of the State Department; the latter is responsible
both for issuing passports and for dealing with loss of citizenship. The
petitioner argued that this section violated both the Due Process Clause
of the Fifth Amendment and his constitutional right of citizenship as
provided by the Fourteenth Amendment, which states that "all persons
born or naturalized in the United States . . . are citizens of the United
States," and that therefore their citizenship could not be legally shifted,
canceled, or diluted. In other words, Afroyim claimed that Congress
does not have the right to revoke citizenship; on the contrary, citizenship could be lost only if the citizen voluntarily renounced it.

Afroyim was thereby contesting the Court's decision in *Perez v.*
Brownell[13] (delivered on the same day as *Trop v. Dulles*) which upheld
the legality of Section 401(e) of the Nationality Act of 1940. In *Perez*
v. Brownell, it was established that Clemente Martinez Perez, a native-
born American who remained outside the United States to avoid military service and voted in elections in Mexico, could lose his citizenship.
In *Trop v. Dulles*, however, the Court decided that expatriation could
not be employed as a punishment. The five-to-four vote in both cases
reveals the sharp divide in the Supreme Court, which was not able to
establish a decisive opinion on whether expatriation was permissible or
not.[14] In the end, the Court ruled that Afroyim's citizenship could not be
revoked without his consent. Noting the special bond between Americans and their government, a bond that protects every citizen against
all manner of destruction of his or her rights, the Court held that only
citizens themselves may voluntarily relinquish their citizenship. This
sacred principle applies equally to native-born and naturalized citizens.
As such, Section 401(e) violated both the Fifth and Fourteenth Amendments and was declared unconstitutional.

According to Aleinikoff, Martin, and Motomura,[15] the ruling in *Af-*
royim v. Rusk was called into question several years later in *Rogers v.*
Bellei[16] partly because two justices had retired and the balance of the
Court had shifted. The case involved Aldo Mario Bellei, who was born
in Italy in 1939 to an Italian father and an American mother and acquired both Italian and American citizenship at birth. In the 1960s, he
was notified that he had lost his U.S. citizenship under a provision of the
Immigration and Nationality Act (1952) that stated that a foreign-born

American would lose his or her citizenship unless he or she moved to the United States and lived there for at least five years between the ages of fourteen and twenty-eight. Bellei argued that according to *Afroyim*, Congress lacked the power to deprive him of citizenship. The majority ruled for the government, upholding the validity of the residency rule.[17] Nevertheless, in 1978, Congress chose to repeal (but not retroactively) all conditions regarding children born abroad to American parents, including the above-mentioned post-acquisition residence requirement.[18] Currently only the parents who want to transfer their American citizenship to their children have residence requirements. This restriction was introduced in order to avoid the indefinite perpetuation of the *jus sanguinis* principle by giving citizenship to co-ethnics who have lost touch with their American roots.

According to Section 349(a)(2) of the Immigration and Nationality Act (1952), an American citizen will lose citizenship by "taking an oath or making an affirmation or other formal declaration of allegiance to a foreign state or a political subdivision thereof." Laurence J. Terrazas, a native-born American, was also the son of a Mexican citizen. In the fall of 1970, at the age of twenty-two, while in Monterrey, Mexico, he applied for a certificate of Mexican nationality. Part of the process required him to make an oath of submission to the Mexican Republic. Consequently, the U.S. Department of State issued a certificate revoking his American nationality, claiming that Terrazas had voluntarily relinquished his U.S. citizenship.

In 1980, the Supreme Court held in *Vance v. Terrazas*[19] that the United States had not only to prove the expatriating act (in this case, Terrazas' taking an oath to a foreign state), but also to demonstrate an intent on the appellee's part to renounce his United States citizenship. Terrazas should not lose his citizenship. However the Supreme Court did not offer guidance for determining which of the various formulations of intent would satisfy the newly recognized intent requirement.[20] The lack of explicit guidelines will be evident in the analysis of the Board of Appellate Review in the next chapter.

An interesting case that exemplifies this provision is the stripping of Rabbi Meir Kahane's American citizenship for assuming a seat in the Israeli parliament in 1984. Contrary to the expatriation policy, which, since the nineteenth century, gave great importance to the spoken word in assessing intent, as the oath, but in agreement with the popular understanding of the meaning of actions,[21] the Courts in the United States agreed that actions speak louder than words. The State Department based its action on section 349(a)(4)(A) of the Immigration and Nationality Act (INA), which maintains that an American will lose his or her American nationality for "accepting, serving in, or performing the duties of any office, post, or employment under the government of a foreign state . . . if he [or she] has or acquires the nationality of such foreign state."[22] Rabbi Kahane appealed to the State Department's Board of Appellate Review. On May 1, 1986, the board in *In re Kahane* affirmed the administrative determination of loss of citizenship.

As a legal scholar, Aleinikoff[23] tried to determine whether stripping Rabbi Meir Kahane of his American citizenship for assuming a seat in the Israeli parliament was constitutional or not. Aleinikoff argued that the 1980s' denationalization measures adopted by the U.S. administration could not be supported by the constitutional system (at least by implication, as the Constitution does not directly address the question of revocation of citizenship). The rulings in both *Afroyim*[24] and *Terrazzas*[25] established the intent-to-relinquish test for the denationalization of citizens by the U.S. government. However, none of the Constitution's four possible implicit conceptions of citizenship (as delineated by Aleinikoff) can independently provide justification for the present doctrine. "The rights perspective gets us to the doctrine, but it is internally incoherent. Consent takes us no place. Contract and communitarian theory cannot rule out state power to terminate citizenship against the will of the individual."[26] Aleinikoff was aware of the irony in the conclusion of his theoretical investigation that the Constitution of United States should have provided protection for Meir Kahane from being denationalized; this was precisely the same harm that Kahane advocated inflicting upon Arabs living in Israel.

But in 1987 the United States district court in Brooklyn decided to restore the American citizenship of Kahane because the government had failed to prove that he had intended to relinquish his citizenship. At the same time, the Israeli parliament passed a law that prohibited Knesset members from holding foreign citizenship. Kahane thereupon renounced his American citizenship in order to take a seat in the Knesset. In 1988 the Knesset disqualified Kahane's party (*Kach*) from being elected to the parliament on the grounds that it was racist.[27] At that point, Kahane wanted to regain his American citizenship—and this time, the court was not willing to reinstate his citizenship. Unlike his previous demand to nullify his expatriation, this time his formal renunciation was conclusive evidence of the necessary voluntary assent on the part of Kahane to becoming non-American.[28]

The Reaction of Congress

Since 1954, the legislative branch has taken action mainly in response to developments in the courts and has rarely initiated changes in U.S. expatriation policy. Congress repealed many of the provisions for the loss of citizenship because they were declared unconstitutional by the courts rather than because it underwent an ideological change.

In 1978 Congress introduced HR 13349 to repeal certain sections of Title III of the Immigration and Nationality Act (1952), which addressed the reasons for the loss of American citizenship. Most of the repealed sections had already been declared unconstitutional. Section 349(a)(5), providing for loss of citizenship for voting in a foreign election, was declared unconstitutional in *Afroyim v. Rusk* (1967). Section 349(a)(8), providing for loss of citizenship for desertion in time of war was declared unconstitutional in *Trop v. Dulles* (1958). Section 352, providing for the loss of citizenship by a naturalized citizen through residence abroad, was declared unconstitutional in *Schneider v. Rusk* (1964).

The deliberations in the House (September 19, 1978) and Senate (September 26, 1978) were very brief. In the House, only three representatives desired to speak, and all supported HR 13349, which repealed some of the expatriation measures. In addition to the fact that those provisions were deemed unconstitutional by the Supreme Court, it was argued that this bill would eliminate some of the hardships and inconvenience caused by the existing expatriation laws for Americans who live abroad. The Senate passed HR 13449 immediately with no amendments. However, a few days later, Edward Kennedy (D-MA), who was not able to be present at the original debate, wanted to express his support for the bill. He also wanted to express his desire and that of several other public figures to reform the nationality laws even further. His proposed law, S. 2314, suggested eliminating all legal discrimination with regard to the transfer of citizenship to American children born of mixed parentage overseas

The Department of State, the Justice Department and the congressional Budget Office supported the enactment of this legislation. Like many other congressional measures, the amendment was effective as of the date of enactment and had no retroactive application. Citizens who had lost their citizenship in the past because of this provision did not regain their status. On October 10, 1978, President Carter signed this amendment into law as Public Law 95–432.

In 1980, the Supreme Court held in *Vance v. Terrazas*[29] that the United States had not only to prove the expatriating act, but also to demonstrate intent on the appellee's part to renounce his or her United States citizenship. Only in 1986, however, did Congress change the wording in the Immigration and Nationality Act (1952) to conform to this ruling. Public Law 99–653 made it explicit that in order to result in a loss of citizenship, any expatriating action needed to be performed voluntarily and with the intention of giving up United States citizenship. In addition, some provisions regarding the loss of citizenship were clarified. For instance, previously a person could lose his or her U.S. citizenship through foreign military service (unless the said service was approved in advance by U.S. officials); the new provision required not only that this service should be performed with the intention to relinquish U.S. ties, but also that the person should have served as an officer and/or in a foreign army that was engaged in hostilities against the United States.

The same logic applied to the residence rule regarding naturalized citizens. In the past, residence abroad of a naturalized citizen within five years following naturalization would have resulted in the loss of citizenship (as it was argued that the naturalized citizen never intended to reside permanently in the United States and therefore should not have received American citizenship in the first place). Subsequently, the five-year period was reduced to one year. This requirement was completely repealed in 1994 when President Clinton signed Public Law 103–416.

As in the amendment of 1978, Congress did not express a fundamental acceptance of multiple loyalties as the main reason for repealing the expatriation policies in 1986. Instead, and in in addition to following various court rulings, the main justification given by Congress was the need to promote a more efficient operation of consular officers in their immigration-related duties. In fact, this legislation was unofficially termed "the consular efficiency bill." During fiscal year 1985, officers at more than 140 U.S. consular posts around the world issued more than six million visas and rejected applications for approximately one million more. The purpose of HR 4823 and HR 4444 was "to improve the efficiency of the Immigration and Naturalization Service (INS) by streamlining certain Immigration Service procedures, clarifying various provisions in current law, strengthening the enforcement capabilities of the Service."[30] In other words, the purpose of this legislation was to provide additional means of cutting back unnecessary procedures and maximizing the utility of INS resources.

Congress debated the amendment of the immigration and nationality laws, both on the floor and in the Subcommittee on Immigration, Refugees and International Law. The committee even held a hearing on July 22, 1986, in which representatives, staff, and concerned citizens could voice their opinions regarding HR 4823 and HR 4444. Only two comments were made regarding the change in expatriation policy. The first was by Joan Clark, the assistant secretary of state for consular affairs, who argued that "This proposal brings the language of the Act into accord with its interpretation and application by the Supreme Court." In addition "This would simplify explanations of the law by the Department in response to inquiries from the public, etc."[31] Arnold Leibowitz, on behalf of American Citizens Abroad, made similar remarks. In both cases, the justification for the new proposal that negated the possibility of forced expatriation was only legal and pragmatic. The floor debates on the bills were brief. While the Senate changed Bill 4444 with regard to the judicial process for adoption, it was agreed that these bills were uncontroversial and were passed without delay.

However, Congress did make an improvement that was not instigated by a court ruling. Section 301(b) of Title III of the Immigration and Nationality Act (1952) maintained that persons who are children of American citizens retain their American citizenship only if they are physically and continuously present in the United States for two years between the ages of fourteen and twenty-eight. This was the only remaining residence requirement in order to retain U.S. citizenship. In *Rogers v. Bellei*,[32] the Court upheld the constitutionality of section 301(b), arguing that the narrow class of persons who are United States citizens by virtue of birth abroad, were not "born of naturalized parents in the United States" and thus did not have the same status as other citizens who are protected under the Fourteenth Amendment. The concern was that there would be generations of American citizens residing outside the United States who have little or no connection to the United States. Since section 301(a)(7) provides that United States citizenship can be transmitted only by American citizens who resided for ten years in the United States (with five of these being after the age of fourteen), the Committee on the Judiciary, which proposed this amendment, saw the residence requirement as an inequality that should be removed.

In the same manner, Section 350 of the Immigration and Nationality Act (1952) was repealed. This section required that persons who at birth acquired dual citizenships and who sought the benefits of their foreign nationality as well as resided in that foreign state after the age of twenty-two take an oath of allegiance to the United States. Otherwise, these persons would be expatriated. Congress held that this section was rarely used, not useful, difficult to administer, and had caused considerable confusion within the departments of State and Justice and thus should be removed from the books.

From 1958 on, the United States Supreme Court issued several rulings that revolutionized the exclusive character of citizenship. In most cases, Congress followed in the Court's footsteps and repealed the sections of the law that obliged forcible revocation of citizenship, unless that was the explicit intent of the citizen. From a legal perspective the ultimately decided principle was that Congress does not have the power to denationalize Americans. Nevertheless, the administration of the national order produces many cases of bad fit from the point of view of ordinary people going about their lives. The State Department still had to resolve the predicaments of hundreds of expatriated United States citizens who appealed to reinstate their citizenship, and to deal with many new cases in which the intent of the American citizens was questionable. Those appeals landed in the hands of the Board of Appellate Review.

7

The Board of Appellate Review

In reaching conclusions about the preponderance of
evidence I think that the Board should take care not to
be misled into simply weighing the quantity of evidence
tending to prove intent as against the quantity of evidence
tending to disprove it.
—Warren E. Hewitt, 1985

Between the years 1980 and 1996, the Board of Appellate Review reviewed
669 contested cases of expatriation. This number includes all appeals
made regarding expatriation (594), motions for reconsideration for those
appeals (52), and several cases regarding the renewal of passports and
immigration (23). Here, I will present statistics on such matters as the
number of cases each year, the grounds for the revocation of citizenship,
and the outcome of the appeal. The limitation of such a report is that it
misses out on the complexities and uniqueness of each deliberation. Each
one of the persons who lost his or her citizenship and appealed to the board
had unique circumstances, gave explanations for his or her deeds, and
made verbal presentations, and members of the board made enormous
efforts to capture these in their deliberations. For this reason, I also
describe in depth several of the cases and present the different elements
that persuaded the board members to affirm or reverse the administrative
decision of expatriation. My aim is not to question any specific decision
made by the board members but to identify the underlying assumptions
of the board regarding the idea of citizenship, and more specifically the
notion that citizenship ought not to be divided or multiple.

The Supreme Court in *Vance v. Terrazas* (1980) held that in order to take
away citizenship, the government had to prove that the expatriating act was
made with the intent to relinquish U.S. citizenship. Theoretically, this decision should have ended the decades of debates regarding the legitimacy
of forced expatriation. The verdict maintained that only the citizen could

determine whether to cease being American. It was the citizen's intent, not only his or her disloyal or questionable act, which would be the benchmark for any expatriation decision. From a legal perspective, two major questions remained: "What is intent?" and "What acts or statements should be weighed in ascertaining intent?" The Board of Appellate Review was, in practice, the body that formulated the answers to these questions.[1]

The work of the Board of Appellate Review has been discussed in the past in several law journals.[2] Here, I am able to introduce at least three new elements. First, while previous descriptions of the board's actions were undertaken during the 1980s, I am able to analyze the changes in its deliberations and procedures after those dates and especially with respect to the transformations in the understanding of expatriation acts in the Department of State in 1990. Second, by quantifying all the appeals made to the Board of Appellate, I am better able to portray the recurrences and trends in affirming or reversing the Department of State's expatriation decisions, as well as the backgrounds of the individuals who appealed. Lastly, I connect the debates in the board to larger perceptions of citizenship and belonging. That is, I reveal the political philosophies that underpinned the board's legal conclusions.

The Board of Appellate Review's Task

The Board of Appellate Review was set up in 1967 to hear appeals and evaluate decisions made by the State Department. The board had the jurisdiction to hear appeals on a variety of administrative decisions such as the cancellation of passports, contract disputes, and expatriation. However, most of the cases discussed were appeals regarding the revocation of U.S. citizenship. Between 1980 and 1996 the board heard 669 appeals of which the vast majority of cases (96 percent) were to decide whether performing a statutory act of expatriation was done with the intent to relinquish American citizenship. I have complete information on only 456 individuals plus 44 appeals for reconsideration of the decisions made by the Board of Appellate Review regarding expatriation. In most cases the affirmation to reverse the State Department's original decision to revoke American citizenship was unanimous (440 cases). However, in a few cases (16), one of the three members insisted that the board should record his or her dissenting opinion. Proving intent was not always an easy task, and was not always agreed upon by all of the board's members.

One of these instances was in the cases of Jeannette Elizabeth Mollenhauer and her husband, John Anthony Mollenhauer. Both were American citizens by birth. John served in the U.S. Army during the Second World War. In 1975, they decided to move to Canada, and six years later, they acquired Canadian citizenship. The record does not show how the American authorities found out about the naturalization in Canada, but once they did, they asked John and Elizabeth to complete a form regarding this act.

In question 13 the couple were asked if they knew that by obtaining naturalization in a foreign state they might lose U.S. citizenship. John replied "Yes—the United States does not permit dual citizenship." In a later questionnaire for determining intent, John added that they had consulted with a U.S. embassy official in Winnipeg regarding the possible expatriation and understood it was necessary in order to obtain Canadian citizenship. On February 4, 1983, the consulate general at Winnipeg prepared a certificate of loss of nationality, which was approved a month later by the State Department, in the names of Jeannette Elizabeth Mollenhauer and John Anthony Mollenhauer. At the end of the year John and Elizabeth filed an appeal to the Board of Appellate Review.

The first stage of this drama illustrates the typical procedure that U.S. consulates around the world follow. First, consular officials must advise citizens and give information on the consequences that certain acts may have on their citizenship. This can happen before the expatriating acts were committed, or as in the case of the Mollenhauers, sometime afterward.

In 1967, when the Board of Appellate Review was established, there were thirteen statutory expatriating acts: having a subversive political stance; deserting in time of war ($349a9); departing the United States to avoid conscription in time of war ($349a10); obtaining benefits from a foreign country ($350); voting in a foreign election ($401e); establishing residence abroad ($352a2); obtaining naturalization in a foreign state ($349a1, previously $401a, and section 2 in the 1907 act); making an oath of allegiance to a foreign state ($349a2 and previously $401b); serving in a foreign army ($349a3 and $401c); serving in a foreign government ($349a4 and previously $401a); making a formal renunciation abroad ($349a5, previously $349a6 and $401f) or in the United States during war

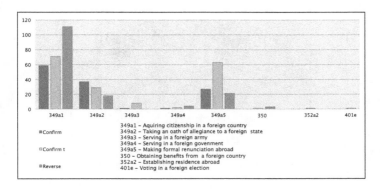

Figure 7.1. Variance in Appeals, 1982–1985

time (§349a7); and committing treason (§349a8). By 1994, the first seven grounds for expatriation were determined to be unconstitutional and were removed from the books. Since 1980, the consulates have informed citizens who committed one of the remaining expatriation acts about the importance of intent, and have allowed citizens to make a declaration of intent just after receiving a notice regarding a certificate of loss of nationality, in order to preserve their American citizenship.

The contrast between descriptive data on the variation in the expatriation acts that were appealed (Figure 7.1) and the reasons for and numbers of expatriations (Figure 7.2) is quite revealing. In Figure 7.1, I describe the three possible outcomes—confirmation of the original decision, reversal of the original decision, and confirmation of the original decision when the board concluded that it is time-barred from ruling on the issue (marked as "confirmed t"). The three most common expatriation acts were acquiring citizenship in a foreign country (§349a1, previously §401a,

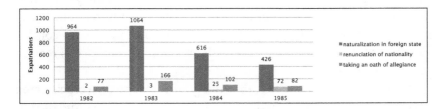

Figure 7.2. Main Reasons for Expatriation, 1982–1985

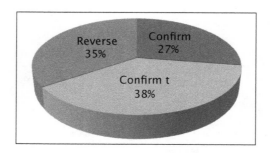

Figure 7.3. Variation in Outcome of Appeals, 1982–1985

and section 2 in the 1907 act); making a formal renunciation abroad (§349a5, previously §349a6 and §401f); and making an oath of allegiance to a foreign state (§349a2 and previously §401b). Those three grounds for expatriation were also the three main reasons for expatriation in all cases (Figure 7.2) in the years 1982–1985.[3] Contrary to the notion that was ruled upon by the Supreme Court, voluntary renunciation of citizenship was not the only reason for the loss of citizenship. It was not even the main reason for the loss of citizenship. In fact, most citizens lost their citizenship without formally, voluntarily, or explicitly requesting to relinquish their American citizenship (either by acquiring another foreign citizenship or by making an oath to a foreign country). Although making a formal renunciation of citizenship is perceived as the ultimate indication for wanting not to be American anymore, more people demanded to keep their citizenship and appealed to the board after performing this act than people who had sworn an oath to foreign country and had lost their citizenship, but desired to retain American citizenship (see Figure 7.1). It was expected that the board would reverse some of the Department of State's decisions to revoke citizenship after the American citizen acquired another foreign citizenship or swore an oath to a foreign country as it could not prove that the act was committed with the intent to relinquish U.S. citizenship. However, it is surprising that the board came to this conclusion in cases when the citizen had made an unambiguous formal request to cease to be American.

Also important is the fact that many of the appeals were rejected because they were time-barred so that the board did not have jurisdiction to rule in those cases. In general, in 35 percent of the appeals, the board agreed with the appellants' request to retain their American citizenship and reversed their original loss of citizenship (see Figure 7.3).

Locating Intent

The consular office is legally bound to report all known acts of expatriation acts to the State Department. The officers can learn about these acts from the citizens themselves who come to seek advice or request services (such as renewing their American passport) or from the foreign government. In the case of the Mollenhauers, the record does not show how the consulate in Winnipeg learned about their naturalization, but it is suspected that they consulted an attorney who later approached the consulate-general.

After the citizen receives the administrative determination of loss of nationality, he or she can file an appeal in a timely and appropriate manner. Then the Board of Appellate Review needs to assess two issues: whether the State Department can prove that the expatriating act was performed voluntarily, and whether it can show that this act was done with the intent to relinquish United States citizenship.

Jeannette and John conceded that the expatriating act—namely, their naturalization in Canada—was done voluntarily. In September 1981, John was granted a certificate of Canadian citizenship. He explained that he felt living in Canada would improve his employment opportunities and stated that his intentions were "to participate in society as a normal citizen in Canada while I resided there."[4] Jeannette also acquired Canadian citizenship upon her own application on the same date. The Mollenhauers did not try to rebut the fact that the statutory act of expatriation was performed voluntarily and the board decided accordingly that the act was undertaken through exercising their free will. The next stage, to show that the Department of State had fulfilled its burden of proof by a preponderance of the evidence that in voluntarily obtaining naturalization in Canada the appellants had intended to relinquish their United States citizenship, was more difficult.

After reviewing their statements (such as their conversations with the consular officers), their written words (such as the questionnaire they filled in at the consulate), and their actions or failure to act (such as their applications for a U.S. passport and its use, connections with family in the United States, and the filing of U.S. States income tax returns), the board had to decide whether intent to relinquish U.S. citizenship was clearly established. The board's majority (Alan G. James and J. Peter A. Bernhardt) concluded that there was nothing in the record to show that they had obtained a Canadian passport or that they held themselves solely as Canadian citizens. Therefore, the Department of State had not sustained its burden of proof, and thus James and Bernhardt reversed the department's decision of loss of U.S. citizenship.

Warren E. Hewitt, who was the third member of the Board of Appellate Review at that time, did not agree with the majority opinion. In his dissenting opinion in the Mollenhauers case, he argued that "In reaching conclusions about the preponderance of evidence I think that the board should take care not to be misled into simply weighing the quantity of evidence tending to prove intent as against the quantity of evidence tending to disprove it. The critical judgment must be the probative force of the separate pieces of evidence that do exist."[5] That is, the board should look on both the acts and words of the citizen at the time he or she performed the expatriating act, and especially the relevant evidence that indicates intent. Hewitt placed more weight on the Mollenhauers explicit written statements at the time of expatriation that they had been fully aware that their American citizenship might be taken away and that they intended to reacquire this citizenship in the future. The written words were to be taken at face value, and there was no reason to look for nuances. Therefore, in this case, Hewitt was of the opinion that the board must affirm the Department of State's certificate of loss of nationality.

On July 1985, the Department of State moved for reconsideration of cases of the board's decision to reverse the original verdict of loss of nationality. About a quarter of the motions for reconsideration (10) were initiated by the state. All the other (44) were appeals from the individuals who did not agree with the board's conclusion and believed it had overlooked or misread some of the evidence in their case. In the case of the Mollenhauers, the board agreed to reexamine the evidence but concluded that their original decision to reverse the department's determination that the Mollenhauers had expatriated themselves when they obtained naturalization in Canada still stood.

The board's decision to reverse the Department of State's certification of loss of citizenship was not unique when it came to cases where the

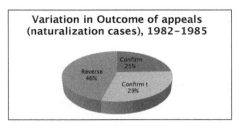

Figure 7.4. Variation in Outcome of Appeals in Naturalization Cases

expatriation act was naturalization in a foreign country and the appeal was made within the required period (usually within one year after the approval by the Department of State of the certificate of loss of nationality or certificate of expatriation). In 38 percent of the cases in general and 29 percent of the cases regarding naturalization, the board maintained that it did not have the jurisdiction to make any decision in the case as they found the appeal time-barred, and therefore dismissed it (see Figure 7.4). Thus, the board affirmed the original ruling of loss of nationality for only a quarter of the cases (in general and in naturalization cases). In cases where the naturalization was in Canada,[6] the board determined in 56 percent of the cases that the state could not prove that the naturalization was made with the intent to relinquish American citizenship. This percentage would probably have been higher if more of the appellants had made their appeal within the required timeframe. In other words, at least in the case of Canada, which can be seen as the least threatening foreign country to the United States, the board did not see eye to eye with the formal regulation that maintained that naturalization in a foreign country should be considered an expatriating act. Becoming a citizen of another country such as Canada was not an indication of the intent to relinquish American citizenship.

Naturalization in a foreign country, taking an oath of allegiance to another state, or performing another act of expatriation may be highly persuasive evidence of intent to terminate U.S. citizenship, but taken alone these are not sufficient to put the issue beyond reasonable doubt. One strategy the Department of State and the Board of Appellate Review have utilized in order to prove intent was to group several expatriating acts together. During the years 1980–1982 the board heard four hundred appeals. In twenty-five of them, the Department of State revoked American citizenship based on at least two of the above expatriating acts. This practice was abandoned after 1982, when most of the expatriation cases came to be determined according to one act of expatriation. However, unofficially, the Department of State continued to justify its decisions in terms of a combination of several expatriating acts.

P. H. Meretsky was a native-born American who moved to Canada with his parents. There, he entered into the practice of law. In 1966 he was informed that he could not qualify for admission to the Canadian Bar and become a solicitor in the province of Ontario while holding American citizenship. On August 31, 1967, Meretsky became a naturalized Canadian citizen in order to practice the profession for which he had trained. In 1976 the United States consulate in Toronto learned that he had become a Canadian citizen when Meretzky came to apply for an American passport. As a result, the Department of State prepared and approved the papers attesting to the loss of his U.S. nationality. Although the revocation of citizenship was based only on section 349a1 (naturalization in a foreign state), the board also looked carefully at another expatriating act—that of taking oath to another country (349a2). Although one can accept that the language of the oath is mainly symbolic, the board took seriously the wording of the oaths taken when becoming naturalized in another country, as well as also upon entering the military or civil service of another country.

The board examined the specific words used in the Canadian oath of naturalization, which in 1967, included the statement that "I hereby renounce all allegiance and fidelity to any foreign person or State of whom or which I may at this time be a subject or citizen. I swear that I will be faithful and bear true allegiance to her Majesty, Queen Elizabeth the Second, Her Heirs and successors according to law and that I will faithfully observe the laws of Canada and fulfill my duties as a

Canadian Citizen so help me God."[7] In the Meretsky case, the board also inspected other acts that might indicate his intent: the documents he used while crossing borders, his failure to inquire about the effect of his impending naturalization on his U.S. citizenship, his representation of himself as an alien in applying for a visa, his establishing his family and his social and professional life solely in Canada, and his answers on a questionnaire filled out at the embassy. Interestingly, the 1976 letter to the board in which he explained that he did not intend to relinquish his U.S. citizenship was not deemed persuasive. This statement was read as subjective and self-serving, and the board affirmed the Department of State's expatriation.

A.B. was born in the United States but moved to Mexico in 1928 when he was one and a half years old. He served in the Mexican Army, but that was not the reason for his loss of U.S. citizenship. Rather, the Department of State decided to revoke his citizenship due his taking an oath of allegiance to Mexico when he entered military service. The Department of State learned about this act by chance when his Mexican military card was discovered during one of his border crossings to the United States and approved his certificate of loss of nationality in 1951. The board did not make any determinations regarding this case as it was filed thirty years after the approval of the certificate of loss of nationality.

In addition to acts that represent intent to relinquish American citizenship, the board also weighed indicators of the intent to remain American, including filing income tax returns; registering for military service; using a U.S. passport; requesting citizenship documentation for children born subsequent to the expatriating act; and participating in social and political life in the United States (including voting). Although being a bad citizen cannot be a reason for the loss of U.S. citizenship, social, political, and even bureaucratic participation in the United States had a significant effect with regard to the determination of intent.

Timed-Barred Indecisions

While debating whether a citizen had performed an expatriating act with the intention to relinquish his or her American citizenship, the Board of Appellate Review also deliberated about appeals that were made beyond the legally mandated time-frame (usually within one year after the approval by the Department of State of the certificate of loss of nationality or certificate of expatriation). That is, while the board did not come to any conclusion regarding the substantive issue of the revocation of citizenship in 38 percent of cases because those cases fell outside the time-frame, the board nevertheless gave in-depth consideration of all the evidence in each appeal, regardless of the period when the expatriating act, the revocation of citizenship, or the issuing of the certificate of loss of nationality took place. Thus, the board discussed the details of most cases, even if the final ruling was that it lacked jurisdiction to affirm or reverse the Department of State's original decision.

It is important to notice that the time limitation was based not on the time that had elapsed between the act of expatriation and the time of appeal, but on the time that elapsed between the issuance of the certificate of expatriation and the filing of the appeal. For example, O.S. was naturalized as a British subject in Canada on February 13, 1937, and therefore expatriated herself under the provision of section 2 of the act of 1907 (later §401a and today §349a1), but the State Department approved the certificate of loss of citizenship only in 1983—forty-six years later. Since the appeal was filed in a timely fashion in the same year, the board did not bar itself from considering this case, agreed with the Department of State's request to reverse its decision, and thus vacated the certificate of loss of nationality.

Emanuel Labes was a native-born American who graduated from Harvard and initially traveled to Palestine to pursue his studies with the prominent archaeologists Nelson Gluck and Sir Flinders Petrie at the American School of Oriental Research in Jerusalem. By 1939, he was among the settlers at Kfar Vitkin, a *moshav* (cooperative agricultural community) in Emek Hefer.[8] In 1941, Labes applied for naturalization in Palestine (which was under British Mandate), arguing that he wanted to fight Nazi Germany. At the time, the United States was not at war with Germany, and as a Jew, he could not enlist in the British armed forces unless he became a Palestinian citizen. Hence his doing so, after which Labes enlisted in the Royal Artillery. The British informed the consular officer in Jerusalem about the expatriating act of naturalization, and in October 1941 the consular officer prepared a certificate of loss of United States nationality. In 1980, Labes appealed to the board to have his United States citizenship reinstated.

The basic issue that the Board of Appellate Review confronted was whether an appeal entered nearly forty years after the statutory act of expatriation occurred could be considered. Labes' counsel argued that it should not be time-barred because the Department of State failed to notify Labes in 1942 of the issuance of the certificate of loss of nationality and he learned about it only when he visited the American embassy in Tel Aviv to apply for a passport. Therefore, according to his counsel, Labes' appeal was entered in a timely manner (less than a year later), and so the board had jurisdiction in this case.

First the board deliberated about the appropriate time-frame that should be applied and whether to accept Labes' appeal. In 1942, the Board of Appellate Review did not exist and therefore Labes could not have appealed to it. A board of review in the passport division did exist, however, and although it was not an appellate review, it did discuss hardship arose from the Nationality Act of 1940. It appears that no forms or procedures regarding this board's work were ever published by the Department of State. A Foreign Service communication from 1949 stated that an appeal could be made, but there was no prescribed time limitation.

With the establishment of the Board of Appellate Review in 1967, it was determined that an appeal of loss of nationality should be made within a "reasonable time" (which was not specified). This procedure was in place until it was amended in 1979. The board decided that in Labes' case, the time limitation that should apply was the one that was in effect prior to 1979. They also were willing to assume that Labes really did not receive an official notification in 1942 as the consulate could not locate any evidence that such a letter was sent (whether because it was lost in wartime conditions or because such records were not collected at that time).

The board's next problem was to determine whether Labes had any other kind of notification of his loss of citizenship before 1980. The law imputes knowledge if such knowledge can be acquired with reasonable care and opportunity. In other word, the question was whether Labes had any signals between 1941 and 1979 that his citizenship status might be in question—signals that would have caused any ordinary person to make inquire about his or her status. In this regard, the board concluded that Labes had many reasons to suspect that his American citizenship was in jeopardy. Labes had surrendered his American passport to the consulate in Jerusalem in the summer of 1941 (justified by the fact that the British army did not want to conscript Americans). In 1946 he obtained a U.S. visa in his Palestinian passport and did not attempt to regain his U.S. passport (allegedly because Palestine was in a state of turmoil). Although Labes acquired his Israeli citizenship automatically, he did serve in the Israeli Defense Forces during the war of 1948 and voluntarily obtained an Israeli passport in 1965. In 1968, he applied again for a visa to travel to the United States. The consulate does have a record of the discussion from that time, and this record clearly shows that Labes knew he might have lost his American citizenship. The board was convinced that although Labes might not have received the original notice of loss of citizenship in 1941, he definitely understood that by 1968. Since he did not take any measures to reestablish his claim to U.S. citizenship until 1979, and since the board could find no compelling reasons for this eleven-year gap, the board concluded that Labes' appeal was not filed in a timely manner and therefore denied it.

After new regulations took effect in 1979, American citizens who lost their citizenship had a time limitation of one year to file their appeal. The board was very stringent in upholding this regulation. Even though it could exercise discretion to extend the time-frame, only rarely was willing it to make a decision regarding expatriation if the appeal was not submitted in a timely manner. This policy corresponds readily with the bureaucratic need to ensure the finality of administrative determinations. All regulations should have a cutoff date, which must be upheld.

For example, D.A.M. was a native-born American. He attended high school in St. Louis, and at the age of seventeen enlisted in the United States Navy. On March 6, 1982, the Department of State determined that he had lost his citizenship by obtaining naturalization in Venezuela by his own application. In a letter dated May 26, 1982, the embassy in Caracas informed D.A.M. of his loss of United States citizenship. On September 5, 1984, D.A.M. entered his appeal to the board.

In the end, the appeal, which was entered two years and six months after D.A.M. expatriated himself, was dismissed as the board concluded that it was time-barred and that they could not consider it. The appellant tried to persuade the board that he did have many mitigating reasons for the delay. He had been hospitalized as a result of two car accidents; his own business was disintegrating; his marriage was under strain and his wife had filed for a divorce; he was under the care of a psychiatrist who treated him for anxiety and stress; and he had had to find temporary employment in Saudi Arabia. The board decided that those circumstances were not beyond his control and could not be justifications "for not taking a moment to assert a timely claim to United States citizenship."[9]

Under the new guidelines, only extreme circumstances would cause the board to allow appeals that were not prepared in a timely manner. This was so in the case of Hesam Hamad Lingawi, who was an American citizen by birth and was taken to Saudi Arabia by his mother when he was three months old. When Lingawi was about to finish high school, his parents reportedly decided that he should attend university in the United States. When they went to apply for a visa, the consular officer in Jidda pointed out that he could not obtain a visa to the United States because he was an American citizen. Although Lingawi had the option to renew his American passport, on November 1977, accompanied by his father, he formally renounced his American nationality.

As mentioned before, the Supreme Court and later the administration (including the Board of Appellate Review and consular officers) were uneasy about the intentions surrounding expatriating acts. However, formally renouncing American citizenship in an embassy or consulate abroad was always understood as a sincere expression of will and thus decisively indicated that the citizen intended to relinquish his or her American citizenship. Thus, Hesam Hamad Lingawi had to convince the board that the expatriation was invalid as it was made involuntarily and that there was a good reason for the five-year delay in the submission of the appeal. The board agreed on both counts.

The board was persuaded that Lingawi was indoctrinated from his early years in the prescription of the Koran in a traditional Muslim state which enshrined the legal code of the Koran—the Sharia—in its domestic code. In such conditions, Lingawi had little room to assert his own free will against that of an authoritative father. Moreover, as long as he was within the economic and religious grasp of his parents, he was constrained from initiating an appeal. It was only after he completed his studies at the University of California at Santa Barbara that he was able to muster up the courage to defy his parents' wishes. Upon consideration of this particular case, the board reversed the Department of State determination that Hesam Hamad Lingawi had expatriated himself when he made formal renunciation of United States nationality in 1977. This can be read as a point made against Islam for the free West; in contrast, when D.A.M.'s life fell apart and he was beset by emotional and financial difficulty, he was held fully responsible.

Although the time limitation was a procedural constraint on the board's work, it did have some theoretical implications. First, the relatively large number of affirmations of the Department of State's original decisions only because of a technical matter signifies that the board did not necessarily agree with its understanding of the idea of expatriation. It only appears that way, as the board had administrative limitations. Second, appealing within a year of the notification of the loss of citizenship may be an indicator of the importance of American citizenship to an individual and signify his or her desire not to relinquish this status. Third, one should question whether the board was really able to accomplish its objective of protecting Americans from forced expatriation.

Legally, the board affirmed two-thirds of the Department of State's expatriation measures. This corresponds to statements made by Alan G. James during an interview for the Foreign Affairs Oral History Collection of the Association for Diplomatic Studies and Training that in "roughly 30% of the nearly 400 cases appealed to the board since 1982 we have reversed the Department and restored citizenship."[10] Nevertheless, the fact that the board reversed only a third of the cases does not necessarily imply that it agreed with the Department of State in the rest of the cases. In 38 percent of the cases, the board did not make a substantive ruling regarding expatriation as it did not have jurisdiction. The percentage is even higher in cases of formal renunciation of American citizenship. We cannot know what would have been the board's affirmation rate if it did not have any time limitations for appeals. In other words, the board explicitly agreed with the Department of State only 27 percent of the time. In all other cases the board reversed the original decision or affirmed it for technical reasons.

A timely filing of the appeal, in addition to being a crucial step toward the reversal of the loss of citizenship, may signify the fact that the citizen does not desire to relinquish his or her American citizenship. Even if at the time that the expatriating act was performed there was intent not to be American anymore, by appealing, the citizen shows that currently he or she does not have such intent. The board did acknowledge this from time to time, but it was not a crucial element in determining its final decision. For example, in the case of W.J.C., who expatriated himself by obtaining naturalization in Australia, the board affirmed the Department of State determination of loss of citizenship. The board "look[ed] in vain in the record for any indication that appellant took any steps, save perhaps, the timely filing of this appeal, to demonstrate that his intention in 1983 was not to relinquish United States citizenship, but to retain it."[11] Therefore, the board concluded that the Department of State did carry its burden of proving that in 1983 the appellant intended to relinquish U.S. citizenship and thus affirmed this decision.

In more than a third of the cases, the board did not seek to determine whether a citizen's expatriating act was carried out with intent to relinquish American citizenship, but instead decided whether the citizen appealed on time. In the summation of the deliberation in the case of W.J.C., the board agreed that ultimately it "cannot penetrate the recesses of an appellant's mind. It must deal with objective evidence of his probable intent. Perhaps appellant did not wish to relinquish United States citizenship, but his words (express renunciation of his allegiance to the United States) and conduct (absence of positive acts to show an objective will and purpose to keep United States citizenship) speak louder than later professions of lack of intent."[12] There is no doubt that from a legal perspective, the state must look at evidence to determine its conclusions. However, from a philosophical perspective, it is not clear that in the mind of the citizen, he did not wish to remain American. One thing is certain, all the citizens who appealed to the board wanted to keep their American citizenship; otherwise, they would not have appealed.

Making a formal renunciation of citizenship is perceived as the ultimate indication for wanting not to be American any more. Only in rare cases did the Board of Appellate Review decide to reverse the voluntary expatriation of an American. Figure 7.1 shows that the board reversed the revocation of citizenship in less than 20 percent of the cases in which citizens requested to remain American after formally renouncing their citizenship. Free will is culturally deemed imperative in the United States, and the members of the board shared this ideal.

Therefore, renunciation should be seen as an explicit, unambiguous, and final expression of wanting to cease being American. Pleas of coercion must be supported by detailed evidence, and economic duress is not a legitimate excuse for such coercion. However, the board did reverse some of the State Department's certifications of renunciation. About half of the reversed renunciations concerned members of the Black Hebrew community.

Between 1973 and 1990, approximately four hundred members of the Original African Hebrew Israelite Nation of Jerusalem, a cult also known as the Black Hebrews or the Hebrew Israelite Community, renounced their American citizenship. Upon leaving the cult, some former members of the Black Hebrew community requested to have their U.S. citizenship restored. Some of the cases were deemed time-barred, but others were accepted. In 1990, the board dealt with eight cases. It decided to restore citizenship in five cases, and rejected the other three. Later that year, the board revisited those three cases and concluded that the renunciation had been psychologically forced and hence reversed its prior decisions.[13]

Although these decisions were well established within legal principles and terminology, they also reveal an important underlying assumption regarding voluntarism and citizenship. The three cases in which the board had initially rejected that argument that renunciation was coerced involved men, while the five cases in which renunciation was deemed involuntary involved a very young man and four women. As was described in Chapter 3, at the beginning of the twentieth century women's citizenship was dependent on their husbands, and they lost their citizenship upon marriage to foreign men. Culturally and legally, women were not seen as independent individuals. This legal barrier was lifted with the Cable Act of 1922, but the cultural discrimination still lingers (although not to the same extent). Children and women can be seen as semi-citizens.[14]

To sum up, the Board of Appellate Review, between the years 1967 and 1991, served as a quasi-judicial division of the U.S. State Department. However, in addition to reviewing appeals, it set the standards for locating intent for expatriation by American citizens. The debates within the board were similar to the dilemmas that consular and diplomatic officers faced at the beginning of the twentieth century (see Chapter 3). That is, the members of the board had to interpret expatriation law and apply it to actual citizens. They had to determine whether an expatriating act was executed with the intention of relinquishing American citizenship.

In contrast to perspectives on citizenship at the turn of the twentieth century, the board had to include Supreme Court decisions that took away power from the State Department to forcibly revoking citizenship and shifted the responsibility to the individual citizen. In this respect, the board's rules of engagement were much more liberal. Then, again, the authority of the board to make exceptions was much more limited. In the late nineteenth century, there was no legislation regarding expatriation. A norm existed, but there were no official guidelines. Therefore the State Department decided on many exceptions relating to the accepted standards at the time. As mentioned in Chapter 3, the consular and diplomatic officers were able to conclude that medical, religious, and economic duress were legitimate reasons for not returning to the United States. In addition, there were no regulations about time limitations constraining the work of the United States representatives abroad. In contrast, with the institutionalization and bureaucratization of the State Department and expatriation law, the Board of Appellate Review was not able to make such exemptions. Moreover, the social norms at the end of the twentieth century were different. Individual stresses such as financial or health troubles were no longer seen as legitimate reasons for taking another citizenship. In the same manner, serving as a church missionary could no longer be an excuse for becoming a citizen of a foreign country. For example, in 1934 Blandine Isabelle Levesque, a native-born American citizen, joined the Sisters of Charity of Montreal and moved to Canada to do missionary teaching. In order to obtain a proper teaching certificate, she was required to take British citizenship. In 1949 the State Department approved her certificate of loss of citizenship for obtaining naturalization in a foreign state. In the beginning of the twentieth century, when missionary work was perceived as being much more important, her religious work would have prevented her from being expatriated. Since Levesque appealed only in 1984, the board was barred by the passage of time from entertaining the appeal, and her Christian missionary work was not a mitigating factor. At the end of the twentieth century, forced expatriation was prohibited, but so was the ability to make exceptions. The national world order had accreted into a bureaucratic norm, whereas at an earlier stage it was more a direct consequence of principle.

New Standards

Although the position that dual nationality could not be a reason for expatriation was expressed in the Supreme Court ruling in *Vance v. Terrazas* (1980), it was only in 1990 that the Department of State issued instructions that clearly stated this principle. In April 1990, all the diplomatic and consular outposts were informed by telegram of a new standard whereby there was a presumption that citizens who obtained naturalization in a foreign state, made declarations of allegiance to a foreign state, or accepted a non-policy position in a foreign state nevertheless intended to retain their American citizenship. The telegram stated that "Changes in interpretation of citizenship law have made [loss of citizenship] cases progressively more difficult to manage. . . . [I]n the past, we have responded to this challenge with more officer time, closer supervision and extra training. At this point, however, we must look to substantial changes in the process if we are to provide equitable, timely and defensible decisions."[15] Although the telegram acknowledged that there were new legal interpretations of expatriation, it did not indicate that they involved explicit acceptance of multiple national allegiances. In September 1990, the new policy was made public in an information sheet entitled "Advice about Possible Loss of U.S. Citizenship and Dual Nationality."[16]

Since the end of the twentieth century, "U.S. citizens who naturalize in a foreign country; take a routine oath of allegiance; or accept non-policy level employment with a foreign government need not submit evidence of intent to retain U.S. nationality. In these three classes of cases, intent to retain U.S. citizenship will be presumed."[17] Although naturalization in a foreign country, taking a routine oath of allegiance, or accepting non-policy level employment with a foreign government are still considered expatriating acts, American citizenship is protected unless those acts are accompanied by the citizen's expressed intention of relinquishing U.S. citizenship.

Moreover, there are no prescribed procedures for administrative appeal of issuance of a certificate of loss of nationality and no mandatory administrative review procedure prior to resorting to judicial processes. Nevertheless, the State Department can at its discretion review determinations of loss of nationality and reconsider them at the request of citizens. Such reconsideration, which is not limited by time, can occur if (1) the law under which the finding of loss was made has been held unconstitutional; (2) a major change in the interpretation of the law of expatriation is made as a result of a U.S. Supreme Court decision; (3) a major change in the interpretation of the law of expatriation is made by the State Department, or by a court or another agency and adopted by the department; and/or (4) the person presents substantial new evidence, not previously considered, of involuntariness or absence of intent at the time of the expatriating act. That is, the department is not timed-barred for reversing past expatriations that would not occur if the expatriating act had been committed today.

At the time this book was written, the progressive acknowledgement of dual citizenship was accepted by all the branches of the U. S. government. The Supreme Court ruled that expatriation can only be a consequence of the citizen's intent not to be American. Congress repealed most of the legislative measures that called for forced expatriation. By 1990, even the State Department had officially recognized that acquiring dual citizenship or acts that represent obtaining another national loyalty cannot, barring the citizen's intent, result in the revocation of American citizenship. From a practical (legal) perspective, dual citizenship is allowed, while forced expatriation is not. In the next chapter we will see that from a sociological perspective, it is still legitimate to propose forced expatriation, especially when connected to the ongoing War on Terror.

The War on Terror

But when you join a foreign terrorist organization as designated by the United States Department of State, that's not your freedom of association . . . and I think when you do that you've essentially said: "I don't want to be an American citizen anymore."
—Senator Joseph Lieberman, 2010

While several years passed until Congress implemented the Court's perspective on expatriation, it took even longer for the administration to recognize and implement the changing interpretation of expatriation policies that the Supreme Court and Congress had expressed. When Congress repealed most of the grounds for expatriation, and more importantly, followed the Court and established that citizenship cannot be taken away without the consent of the citizen, it changed more than a bureaucratic lacuna. Henry Ansgar Kelly, who studied State Department leaflets, came to the conclusion that the recognition of dual citizenship was formally introduced to consular offices around the world only in 1990. However, this shift does not represent a philosophical transformation but a practical acknowledgment of this status. As Secretary of State James Baker explicitly asserted in a telegram of April 1990 in regard to Americans having dual citizenship, "This action should not be seen as an endorsement of dual nationality."[1]

Today, the United States tolerates dual citizenship on the part of the millions of Americans who have it. Unlike courts in the past, courts today maintain that actions that indicate dual or split allegiance or even the abandonment of American allegiance are not sufficient for compulsory expatriation. The state has to prove that any act of expatriation on the part of a citizen was performed voluntarily and with the intention to relinquish American citizenship. Nevertheless, it is questionable whether Americans have really adopted a political philosophy that embraces multiple national loyalties.

The ideal of perpetual allegiance was done away with by the American Revolution. Throughout the nineteenth century and the beginning of the twentieth, the United States fought to export the notion of naturalization in both domestic laws and international treaties. National allegiance could shift from one country to another. However, citizenship was still perceived as an exclusive status and loyalty was expected to be given to a single nationality. As the previous chapters suggest, it appears that modern citizenship is shifting again.

Toleration of Dual Citizenship

The changes in the United States Supreme Court since *Trop v. Dulles* (1958), the subsequent repeals of many of the legislative measures regarding expatriation, and finally the 1990 written acknowledgement by the Department of State that expatriating acts are not to be taken as indications of the intent to relinquish citizenship, all suggest that in the United States divided and multiple national loyalties have become acceptable. As Spiro maintains, "Recent trends toward acceptance of the status [of dual citizenship] reflect the erosion of the allegiance paradigm,"[2] which has now been replaced by a residence paradigm. Today, we are experiencing the consolidation of a new stage in the history of citizenship.

The many studies of the acceptance of dual citizenship around the world reinforce this perspective. Martin argues that the current conditions of globalization, peace, complex identities, an effective human rights regime, and expanding democratization all make dual citizenship more likely and more acceptable.[3] Blatter, Erdmann, and Schwanke[4] present the combined empirical data gathered by the United States Office of Personnel Management, along with the studies of several other citizenship scholars.[5] All of these studies show that acceptance of dual citizenship has been rising steadily since the Second World War. Moreover, the trend is towards an expansive and nonexclusive notion of citizenship.

Spiro argues that the acceptance of dual citizenship is another stage, and may be the most dramatic one, in the diminishing of American national identity in the face of globalization. While in the past "dual nationality was not merely unacceptable. It was an abomination,"[6] today it is not unusual, problematic, or freakish to hold more than one citizenship. The United States tolerates dual citizenship, and it is improbable that this trend will change in the future.

This viewpoint was also presented by David Martin. "With the end of the Cold War, and a host of other developments that promote a more tightly linked, more peaceful, and more democratic globe, it is indeed time to reconsider the classic aversion to dual nationality, and to eliminate some of the rules and practices that have constricted it."[7] Martin envisioned a new world order that embraces dual citizenship and multiple national allegiances. I do not dispute such standpoints that portray the growing acceptance of dual citizenship, but I do call on us to be cautious in such declarations. Throughout the book, I have shown how entrenched is the notion of exclusive national loyalty in the minds of administrators and legislators (although the matter was overruled long ago by the Supreme Court). Moreover, even if we do agree that substantial change in the perception of dual nationality has occurred since the end of the Cold War and in the face of globalization, the War on Terror signifies how fragile and temporary this transformation can be.

The Re-Emergence of Exclusive National Allegiance

On the morning of September 11, 2001, terrorists attacked America without warning. In a series of coordinated suicide attacks, nineteen Al-Qaeda terrorists hijacked four commercial passenger jet airliners and crashed them into the Twin Towers of the World Trade Center in New York City, the Pentagon in Arlington, Virginia, and a field near Shanksville in rural Pennsylvania, killing altogether 2,923 individuals. The overwhelming majority of casualties were civilians, including nationals of over seventy countries. The impact of those attacks on the United States and on the entire world was immediate and dramatic. The very next day, President Bush declared war on terrorism. A month later, President Bush signed into law the USA Patriot Act, giving law enforcement agencies expansive powers and increased resources to fight terrorism at home and abroad. In response to the attacks, the United States also invaded Afghanistan (in 2001) and Iraq (in

2003). Those wars created new conditions in which American citizens could become involved in terrorism against the United States. In the view of many, such Americans manifested in those acts their rejection of the United States and therefore deserved to have their citizenship rescinded. However, the current expatriation statutes do not provide for the revocation of citizenship in cases where an American serves in a hostile foreign terrorist organization. They thus fail to take account of the myriad ways in which, in the modern world, war can be waged against the United States. Thus, the administration wanted to change its expatriation policies.

On February 7, 2003, a confidential draft of the Domestic Security Enhancement Act of 2003, more commonly known as Patriot Act II, was released to the public by the Center for Public Integrity. A month earlier, the Bush administration had prepared this bold, comprehensive sequel to the USA Patriot Act passed in the wake of September 11, 2001, which would have given the government, in the name of anti-terrorism, sweeping new powers to increase domestic intelligence-gathering, sur-veillance, and law-enforcement prerogatives, and simultaneously de-crease judicial review and public access to information.[8] In connection with expatriation, this provision would have amended 8 U.S.C. Section 1481 to make clear that just as an American can relinquish citizenship by serving in a hostile foreign army, so can he or she relinquish citizenship by serving in a hostile terrorist organization.

Title V: Enhancing Immigration and Border Security
SEC. 501: EXPATRIATION OF TERRORISTS.
Section 349 of the immigration and Nationality Act (8 U.S.C, 1481) is amended—(1) by amending subsection (a)(3) to read as follows:
"(3)(A) entering, or serving in, the armed forces of a foreign state if—
"(i) such armed forces are engaged in hostilities against the United States; or
"(ii) such person serves as a commissioned or non-commissioned of-ficer, or
"(B) joining or serving in, or providing material support (as defined in section 2339A of title 18, United States Code) to, a terrorist organization designated under section 212(a)(3) or 219 or designated under the International Emergency Economic Powers Act, if the organization is

engaged in hostilities against the United States, its people, or its national security interests." And

(2) by adding at the end of subsection (b) the following: "The voluntary commission or performance of an act described in subsection (a)(3)(A)(i) or (B) shall be prima facie evidence that the act was done with the intention of relinquishing United States nationality."[9]

Specifically, Section 501 maintained that an American could be expatriated if he or she became a member of a group that the United States has designated a "terrorist organization" (or provided support to such a group) if that group was engaged in hostilities against the United States. In other words, this proposed legislation would have reinstated in the United States the practice of revoking citizenship as a punishment. This law would also have criminalized any material support for terrorism, even if perpetrated unknowingly.[10]

However, more significant is the fact that this provision would also make explicit the notion that the intent to relinquish nationality did not need to be manifested in words, but could be inferred from conduct. The Supreme Court had already recognized that intent could be inferred from conduct, arguing in *Vance v. Terrazas* that the "intent to relinquish citizenship . . . [can be] expressed in words or . . . found as a fair inference from proved conduct." In *King v. Rogers* (1972) it was argued that "specific subjective intent to renounce United States citizenship . . . may [be] prove[n] . . . by evidence of an explicit renunciation, acts inconsistent with United States citizenship, or by affirmative voluntary act[s] clearly manifesting a decision to accept [foreign] nationality." In *United States v. Schiffer* (1993) it was maintained that "Specific intent may . . . be proven by evidence of what steps the alleged expatriate did or did not take in connection with his expatriating acts."[11] In contrast to current interpretation of the Constitution and expatriation law, this proposal would make service in a hostile army or terrorist group *prima facie* evidence of intent to renounce citizenship.

After the Center for Public Integrity posted the proposed changes to the USA Patriot Act, Barbara Comstock, director of public affairs for the Justice Department, released a statement saying that this was an early draft that did not represent the administration's position. Eventually, the bill drafted by the Justice Department in 2003 never reached Congress.

Opponents of the Bush administration claimed that this bill showed the true face of the government. David Cole, a Georgetown University law professor, reviewed the draft legislation. His response was that the text "raises a lot of serious concerns." This proposed law, he added, "would radically expand law enforcement and intelligence gathering authorities, reduce or eliminate judicial oversight over surveillance, authorize secret arrests, create a DNA database based on unchecked executive 'suspicion,' create new death penalties, and even seek to take American citizenship away from persons who belong to or support disfavored political groups." Cole found it disturbing that there had been no consultations with Congress on the draft legislation. "It . . . is troubling as a generic matter that they have gotten this far along and tell people that there is nothing in the works. What that suggests is that they're waiting for a propitious time to introduce it, which might well be when a war is begun. At that time there would be less opportunity for discussion and they'll have a much stronger hand in saying that they need these right away."[12] Proponents of the bill in the Bush administration claimed that this draft was not meant to be legislated, but that the Justice Department had only wanted to explore and gauge different alternatives to the current laws.

Regardless of the evaluation of the government, it is evident that many people still hold the belief that some actions against the United States should be punished by expatriation. It is true that the failure of the proposal to get anywhere implies that there is not great support for forced expatriation in the United States. Nevertheless, from a sociological point of view, it is important to point out that this proposal was legitimate enough to be formulated. Taking away citizenship from citizens who have committed treason is not new or unique to the United States. Treason is not only an abhorrent crime that deserves extreme punishment, but might be the ultimate expression of transfer of national allegiance. Although legally expatriation should not be a punishment for criminal offenses, it is commonly understood that committing treason against one's country clearly signifies intent to relinquish one's nationality.

Therefore, it was a legitimate compromise to release Yaser Esam Hamdi, an American who fought with the Taliban in Afghanistan against U.S. soldiers, to Saudi Arabia without charge on the condition that he renounce his U.S. citizenship. Although the courts could not establish that his actions were carried out with the intention of relinquishing his American citizenship, and although expatriation ought not to be a punishment for any deviant behavior, it was accepted that taking away Hamdi's American citizenship was an appropriate and legitimate measure. It was not perceived that Hamdi was thereby able to evade punishment.

In 2004, the United States of America, by and through its representatives, and Yaser Esam Hamdi agreed that although "Hamdi has performed an expatriating act under Section 349(a) of the Immigration and Nationality Act, it has not been adjudicated."[13] Nevertheless, "Hamdi agrees to appear before a diplomatic or consular officer of the United States at the United States Embassy in Riyadh, Saudi Arabia, and formally to renounce any claim that he may have to United States nationality pursuant to Section 349(a)(5)." It was also maintained that that the United States still has a right "to determine that Hamdi lost United States nationality at an earlier time."

Yaser Esam Hamdi was not the first American to be stripped of his American citizenship in exchange for his freedom. Tomoya Kawakita, born in the United States to Japanese parents, had dual American and Japanese citizenship. He was in Japan when the Second World War broke out. Because of the war, he was unable to return to the United States. During the war, he actively supported the Japanese cause, and as a civilian interpreter in the prison camp at Oeyama, Kawakita, known as "The Meatball," abused and tormented American prisoners of war who had been forced to work under him. After the war, he returned to the United States on a U.S. passport and started graduate studies at the University of Southern California. While in a store in Los Angeles, Kawakita was recognized by William Bruce, a former prisoner of war, who reported Kawakita to the authorities. The Federal Bureau of Investigation arrested Kawakita in June 1947, and he was indicted on fifteen counts of treason for his wartime activities.

Kawakita claimed that he had lost his U.S. citizenship by registering in Japan as a Japanese national during the war, and as a result he could not be found guilty of treason against the United States. Presumably, the reason Kawakita fought so tenaciously not to be considered a U.S. citizen was that he saw this as the only way to escape a death sentence for his conviction of treason.

However, the Supreme Court ruled that since Kawakita had dual nationality by birth, when he registered himself as Japanese, he was simply reaffirming a preexisting fact and was neither actually acquiring Japanese citizenship nor renouncing his American citizenship. Since Kawkita had committed hostile acts as an employee of a Japanese corporation, not the Japanese army, he was deemed to have retained his United States citizenship. Although Kawakita lost his appeal, his death sentence was eventually commuted by President Eisenhower. President Kennedy, in one of his last official acts before his assassination, ordered Kawakita released on the condition that he be stripped of U.S. citizenship, deported to Japan, and never be permitted to return. As in the case of Hamdi, the administration could not accept divided allegiance. In both cases, the state preferred to revoke the citizenship of treacherous Americans and deport them rather than to punish them as Americans in the United States.

Although the current U.S. laws do not permit expatriation to be used as a punishment, several court rulings suggest that revocation of citizenship may still have punitive aspects. In *Fedorenko v. United States* (1981), the government sought to denaturalize Feodor Fedorenko for misrepresenting in his 1949 visa application the fact that he served during the Second World War as an armed guard at the Nazi extermination camp of Treblinka in Poland. Acknowledging that Fedorenko had been forced to serve as a guard, the district court dismissed the government claim to cancel his citizenship. However, the Fifth Circuit Court of Appeals reversed this decision, arguing that Fedorenko was able to obtain U. S. citizenship only by concealing information about his past, and therefore it was automatically subject to revocation.[14]

The case of Josias Kumpf was similar. Kumpf was denationalized for failing to state in his immigration forms from 1956 that he had served in the Waffen S.S. during the Second World War.[15] In 2002, the government sought to revoke the American citizenship of Lionel Jean-Baptiste who was convicted of conspiring to distribute cocaine in 1995 and subsequently served his sentence. However, the government claimed that he had illegally obtained his citizenship by committing unlawful acts before his application for citizenship was approved. Both the district court and the Eleventh Circuit ruled in the government's favor.[16] The above cases exemplify that even when punitive revocation of citizenship is eliminated from the law books, *de facto* such an option still exists. For this reason, Ronner accused the judicial system of being "purely ministerial, entailing a rubber-stamping of an order of naturalization."[17]

Expatriation as Punishment

Expatriation laws do consistently respond to the overt manifestation of massive disloyalty (which has had various delineations at different times). Although the meaning of disloyalty is different in each country or period, taking away citizenship is clearly one of the policing measures for such behavior. Expatriation has been perceived as a punishment. Between 1865 and 1958 stripping away citizenship was given legal justification and was implemented as a response to a specific "deviant" action.[18] Although the law today does not permit the use of expatriation as punishment, it is still associated with an undesired action of the citizen. The fact that a policy of forced expatriation is illegal does not eliminate the social legitimacy of taking away citizenship from some Americans considered unworthy of it.

Historically, 1954 was the last time new grounds for expatriation were enacted. Nevertheless, such legislation has been considered since and might be developed in the future. For example, the draft Domestic Security Enhancement Act, informally known as Patriot Act II, included a provision to strip citizenship from anyone who materially supported (even indirectly) activities of organizations that the executive branch deemed "terrorist." Today, such activities are grounds only for criminal prosecution, not for the loss of citizenship.[19] Nevertheless, the Hamdi case, presented above, illustrates that citizenship can be removed actually, albeit sometimes indirectly as part of the War on Terror, regardless of current interpretation of the Constitution. It is apparent that expatriation is still associated both with punishment and armed conflict.

On May 6, 2010, Senator Joseph Lieberman (I-CT) introduced the Terrorist Expatriation Act, which would make "engaging in . . . hostilities against the United States" or "providing material support or resources to a foreign terrorist organization" grounds for revoking a person's citizenship.[20] While Senator Lieberman's bill was being cosponsored by Senator Scott Brown (R-MA), Representatives Jason Altmire (D-PA) and Charlie Dent (R-PA) introduced the same bill in the House. The move came days after Faisal Shahzad—a Pakistani-American who was a naturalized U.S. citizen—was arrested in connection with a failed plot to set off a bomb in New York City's Times Square. The bill was intended to add terrorism to the list of expatriating acts in section 349 of the Immigration and Nationality Act. As in the Hamdi case, this proposal brought with it a set of disturbing questions regarding the rights of Americans. For example, the bill added "material support" for terrorism to the list of actions that can result in loss of citizenship, although it is unclear what this provision included. It was also unclear whether suspected terrorists would have to be convicted in a federal court as a prerequisite for the loss of their citizenship.

During an appearance on Fox News, Senator Lieberman argued that

> it's one thing to belong to a club, even a political group, that I might think is radical here in the United States. . . . But when you join a foreign terrorist organization as designated by the United States Department of State, that's not your freedom of association. You've joined a group, one of whose central purposes is to bring down America, to ruin our security, to change our way of life, and I think when you do that you've essentially said: "I don't want to be an American citizen anymore, whether you intended to say it or not."[21]

However, some commentators maintain that the proposed bill will make little difference in the "war on terror" and it does not accomplish much, except for positioning Senator Lieberman as "tough" on terrorism (and cynics would say that that is a ploy to get more air time on TV). The reason for this minimal effect is that the bill does not change the *Vance v. Terrazas* rule whereby the commission of an expatriating act without being accompanied by the subjective intention to renounce one's citizenship should not result in the loss of citizenship. That is, the bill would not work the way Senator Lieberman's statements assume it would—joining a terrorist group is not the same as saying "I don't want to be an American citizen anymore." Moreover, the new expatriation act would not change the existing due process or the "preponderance of evidence" standard specified by Congress (the government must show the expatriating act was (1) voluntarily committed and (2) "with the intention of relinquishing United States nationality.")

Whether one argues that the proposed expatriation act is a serious violation of civil rights, or just a political maneuver, it is evident that removing citizenship from Americans can be considered an acceptable practice under certain circumstances. Otherwise, Senator Lieberman would not have put his reputation at stake by proposing such a measure. In the end, the session of Congress ended without voting on the bill and it was cleared from the books. The bill has yet to be reintroduced. As with Patriot Act II, Lieberman's bill was not able to secure wide support, not even from all Republicans. Although there are multiple reasons for a bill not to pass, this is a good indication that the ideas expressed by the Supreme Court since 1958, have permeated Congress as well.

While the Supreme Court maintains that taking away citizenship should not be a punishment, nor should it be forced upon a person, some members of Congress and the administration still oppose dual allegiances (the reason for most expatriation provisions) and believe that it is appropriate for some actions against the United States to result in the perpetrator's having his or her American citizenship revoked.

The socio-historical analysis of this book has aimed to follow and understand the logics of the official perception of dual citizenship and the revocation of citizenship. According to several scholars, some political elites, as well as some segments of the public, find the rejection of multiple national allegiances acceptable. For example, Stanley Renshon, a political psychologist, argues that exclusive national loyalty is critical to the American civil process.[22] Glazer argues that that "the average congressman or American will see nothing wrong in insisting on primary loyalty to the United States from new citizens."[23]

Taking away Hamdi's citizenship as retribution for his hostile activities in Afghanistan was perceived as a new step in America's War on Terror. It resulted in a native-born American being expatriated as punishment. Citizenship—the right to have rights—once again became vulnerable. In the current chapter, I have shown that although revocation of citizenship has had a long tradition in the United States, changes in the interpretation of the law have limited the ability of the state to administer this policy. Since expatriation has become dependent on the voluntary consent of the citizen, the State Department has had to find intent in order to strip Americans of their citizenship. I described three mechanisms for this process: coercing the citizen to accept an agreement whereby he or she voluntarily consents to relinquish his or her status; masking the true reason for expatriation and presenting a case that is less controversial; or trying to introduce new laws (like the Patriot Act II or the Terrorist Expatriation Act) that maintain that some actions are *prima facie* evidence of an intent to renounce citizenship. Legally, expatriation is not a punishment. Socially, taking away citizenship in response to un-American behavior was, and in particular circumstances still is, acceptable.

9

Dual Citizenship and the Revocation of Citizenship

13. LOSS OF U.S. CITIZENSHIP Under certain circumstances, you may lose your U.S. citizenship by performing,
voluntarily and with the intention to relinquish U.S. citizenship, any of the following acts . . .
—United States Passport

Citizenship in the United States emerged in the eighteenth century
in response to British treatment of national allegiance as singular and
perpetual. While the United States advocated for transferable loyalty, it,
too, was suspicious of divided national loyalty. Thus, the United States
enacted grounds for expatriation in order to regulate the exclusive
nature of nationality. Transnational immigration, changes in national
and international norms, and new interpretations of dual citizenship
domestically gradually led the United States to adopt a lenient and
pragmatic policy regarding dual citizenship. However, the War on Terror
brought back some of the exclusive notions of citizenship (even if they
were not put into practice). Judicial interpretations of the Constitution
that prohibit the use of expatriation policies do have an effect on
our conception of the world. However, it is immediate (political and
practical) concerns that shape the stance toward dual national allegiance.
Socially, dual citizenship is still considered by many politicians to be
objectionable, implying a will not to be American—a will that can, in
turn, be seen as un-American.

In this book I have analyzed revocation of citizenship laws in the
United States. In the initial chapters I showed that there is an overarching
principle that has played a role in the perception of citizenship and its
revocation, both in the past and present. Forced expatriation as a policy
became legitimate and widespread with the institutionalization of a
world order that did not tolerate multiple national allegiances.

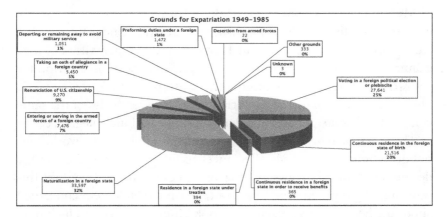

Figure 9.1. Grounds for Expatriation from the United States, 1949–1985. Data compiled from the *Immigration and Naturalization Service Statistical Yearbooks*, between the years 1949 and 1985.

The twentieth century brought numerous changes to our society, including the crystallization of the national world order (and some would say the beginning of its demise). The thesis of this book is based on a comparative analysis of one of the less-acknowledged phenomena in the Western democratic world—that of stripping away citizenship. It is less known because there is an assumption that the status of citizenship in democratic countries is secure and that the revocation of citizenship is associated only with totalitarian or oppressive regimes.[1] In democracies, new (and not only illegal) immigrants are sometimes suspected of dual loyalty, but native-born nationals are usually automatically perceived as loyal. For example, it is said that having been born in the United States makes you 100 percent American. But this is not borne out by the facts. Between 1949 and 1985, more than 100,000 Americans lost their citizenship on various grounds (Figure 9.1). Since the Supreme Court had already removed many of the grounds for forced expatriation during this period, it is reasonable to presume that even more Americans lost their citizenship in between the American Civil War and the Second World War, though such revocations were not recorded by any official American agency. The United States is not unique. Most countries in the world have some variation on statutes that specify grounds for forced expatriation.

My analysis has shown that taking away citizenship is largely dependent on the way dual citizenship is perceived. Under the national world order, multiple national loyalties are not permitted. Thus, acquiring an additional citizenship became the main justification for countries to take away the original citizenship status. Restrictions on dual citizenship and forced expatriation are different sides of the same coin. Both are state policies that demand single national allegiance.

The national logic as an ideal organizing principle for the world cannot accommodate multiple allegiances to different states. During the debates on citizenship laws, politicians and diplomats did not take this possibility lightly. After the Civil War, the United States was concerned about the loyalty of its citizens and took different measures, including forced expatriation, in order to limit multiple national loyalties. From the 1950s onward, however, the three branches of the United States government gradually adopted a more lenient position toward split or divided national allegiances. This transformation was not linear or inevitable. In the nineteenth century, it was the diplomatic and consular officers who established the norms regarding exclusive citizenship. Since the Civil War, Congress' role has been to step in by codifying the existing norms and by enacting new regulations regarding expatriation. Until the Cold War, both the executive and judicial branches followed the lead of the legislators who were in favor of revoking citizenship. Only in 1958 did the United States Supreme Court begin to rule against the constitutionality of forced expatriation. Gradually, the two other branches of government began to recognize the shift in attitude toward dual citizenship. This process culminated in 1990 with the new standard of the State Department that acknowledged that expatriating acts without intent to relinquish American citizenship would no longer result in the loss of American citizenship. Today, the United States tolerates dual citizenship, and it is impossible to lose American citizenship without the individual deliberately intending to abandon his citizenship. However, although diminishing in its influence, the national world order is still hegemonic, and even received some reinforcement after the events of 9/11. Moreover, while the United States tolerates dual citizenship, it has still not formally accepted it. A comparison between Canada and the United States can help show the difference between partial toleration of dual citizenship in the United States and wholehearted embrace of multiple national identities in Canada.

Between Tolerating and Embracing Dual Citizenship

Bloemraad[2] analyzed immigration and naturalization patterns in the United States and Canada and concluded that the public embrace of dual citizenship in Canada has promoted immigration to that country. In contrast to the United States, which does not explicitly allow dual national allegiances, Canada explicitly affirmed its acceptance of dual citizenship in 1977. Bloemraad suggests that acceptance of dual citizenship is associated with limited military conflict. The particular security concerns and histories of nation-building in each country gave rise to greater tolerance for dual citizenship in Canada. The United States was created out of an armed revolution and has since participated in many wars. Under the circumstances, citizenship is perceived as an issue of national security. U.S. expatriation polices have usually been presented (and justified) as the means to prevent dual loyalty of its citizens. Although this law has not been enforced in the past three decades, dual nationality is still officially prohibited in the United States. Until the 1990s, most grounds for taking away citizenship were based on a direct or indirect presumption that the citizen had transferred his or her nationality or desired to do so. This guiding principle can explain why expatriation was common in the United States, while Canada has involuntarily expatriated only thirty-seven people since 1977.

In 1946, the Canadian Citizenship Act of 1946 made Canada the first member of the British Commonwealth to establish a citizenship status distinct from that of the "Mother Country." Until then, both native-born and naturalized citizens were considered British subjects. The current regulations regarding citizenship came into force thirty years later with the Citizenship Act of 1977.

The difference between the two laws regarding the loss of citizenship is a significant one. The Citizenship Act of 1977 is a benchmark for the perception of Canadian citizenship and its loss. Until then, citizenship was associated with fidelity to a single nation and thus could be revoked on many grounds. Subsequent to the 1977 legislation, citizenship was perceived as a natural right that the government could not revoke. That is, prior to 1977, citizenship could be lost on the grounds of acquiring another nationality (other than by marriage), serving in the armed forces of another country, taking an oath or other declaration of allegiance to a foreign county, renouncing Canadian citizenship, or obtaining that citizenship by false representation, fraud, or concealment of material circumstances. In contrast, after 1977, most of these provisions were lifted, and the Canadian government publicly and proudly asserted its embrace of dual citizenship and removed the exclusivity clause from its oath of allegiance. This transformation in Canadian politics can be attributed to the emerging multicultural perspective and to the need to accommodate the duality of its national identity as both Francophone and Anglophone.

According to the 1977 legislation, citizenship can be revoked for only two reasons. One is if it was obtained by false representation, fraud, or knowingly concealing material circumstances. The other concerns second-generation Canadians born abroad, who lose their citizenship when they turn twenty-eight unless they make an application to retain it and produce evidence of living in Canada or having a substantial connection with it. It is important to repeat that between 1977 and 2002, only thirty-seven Canadians lost their citizenship as a result of the first provision. Furthermore, it can be argued that those thirty-seven cases did not constitute revocation of citizenship because the individuals concerned should not have received it in the first place. Thus, the 1977 Citizenship Act in effect articulates the principle that Canadian-born citizens can never forcefully lose their citizenship.[3]

Practically and symbolically, there is a difference between toleration of dual citizenship in the United States and the explicit acceptance of dual citizenship in Canada. Although the end results regarding expatriation may be similar and citizenship is secure in both countries, from a social perspective a distinction should be made.

The example of expatriation in Canada also reinforces my assertion that perceptions about dual citizenship and the revocation of citizenship are likely to fluctuate. Protection against forced expatriation and the acceptance of dual citizenship are deeply rooted in the Canadian citizenship law and cultural perception of Canada as a multi-ethnic country of immigration. But even in Canada, there are voices calling for the re-introduction of the principle of exclusive national allegiance, especially following the American War on Terror.[4]

In 2002, Bill C-18 was introduced to parliament with the intent of establishing new grounds for the revocation of citizenship—security and annulment. Bill C-18 proposed creating a special revocation process for those accused of terrorism, war crimes, or organized crime. In the name of security, this proposal could have had harsh consequences for judicial due process as it allowed the use of protected information, which is disclosed only to the judge and is concealed from the person accused. Moreover, no appeal or judicial review would have been permitted.[5] Both of the above-mentioned revisions to the Citizenship Act would constitute a change to the policy that once Canadian citizenship is acquired it cannot be revoked due to any conduct on the part of the citizen. Due to considerations of due process and citizenship rights, the provisions in the proposed bill were recommended for removal by the Parliamentary Standing Committee on Citizenship and Immigration in 2005.

Justifications for the reversal of the embrace of dual citizenship arose not only from security concerns, but also from concerns with protection of Canadian citizens abroad (similar to the nineteenth-century concerns of American diplomats, discussed in Chapter5). In 2006, following the war between Israel and the Hezbollah in Lebanon, the government of Canada devised plans to evacuate Canadians from Lebanon. Approximately 13,670 of the estimated 40,000 to 50,000 Canadians who were visiting or residing in Lebanon were evacuated[6] in a process that was unprecedented in terms of the effort and the complexities involved. Since many of the rescued Canadians were dual citizens, the evacuation provoked (or rather renewed) the controversy about the status of dual citizenship in Canada and the legal and cultural distinction between "true" citizens who are entitled to protection and dual citizens who are not. While the evacuation was supported by the government, which was committed to protecting all Canadians, by Canadians who cited the importance of transnational economic and cultural networks, and by legal scholars who defended the ideal of dual citizenship, the debate was dominated by opposing voices, which accused the dual citizens of being uncommitted citizens who were abusing the good will of the Canadian tax payers.[7] The national world order was thus implicitly evoked in the attempt to shore up a presumably racially defined Canadian identity by means of identifying an "un-Canadian" and a "non-white" outsider.

It is difficult to infer intentions from inactivity. Nevertheless, the fact that the remaining statutes regarding dual citizenship in the United States are rarely enforced has been taken to signify the acceptance of dual citizenship in America. In the same manner, we can assume that the United States accepts multiple nationalities when it does not take the exclusivity clause in the oath of allegiance seriously. Although naturalized citizens must swear that they renounce all previous national loyalties upon receiving their United States citizenship, the implementation of this promise is never examined by the authorities. Both abovementioned assertions are probably correct. The United States accepts *de facto* dual citizenship. However, the American government has never suggested abolishing the exclusivity section from the oath; nor has it proposed explicitly embracing dual citizenship (as Canada did). The United States has also been loath to repeal sections in the law that still make the revocation of citizenship possible in certain circumstances. Although the United States does allow millions of Americans to hold dual citizenship, it has refrained from taking the extra step of publicly expressing this sentiment. This inertia needs to be addressed.

Every American citizen in the final stage of naturalization has to take the oath of allegiance in which he or she swears to renounce all previous allegiances.[8] Although it is clear that the intention of the oath is to ensure that naturalized citizens abandon their former loyalties, the law does not require new citizens to demonstrate that they are expatriated from their country of origin.[9] In order for the oath to remain meaningful, it would be preferable and more honorable for the renunciation section to be omitted [10] and for the language of the oath to be changed in such a way that precedence is given to the newly acquired American citizenship without requiring that the new citizens renounce their former allegiances[11] or enforcing for the first time the swearing of the oath of renunciation.[12] Neither of these options has been selected.

There is ample evidence that dual citizenship is becoming legally acceptable around the world. Unlike during most of the nineteenth and twentieth centuries, in the twenty-first possessing multiple national allegiances is no longer considered abhorrent. However, this perspective, like most policies, is historically contingent and is not irreversible.

Dual Citizenship and Wars

Citizenship has always been associated with soldiering and military service.[13] This connection can be located on many levels. The social and political construction of citizenship developed with respect to warfare. The granting and expanding of rights was linked to conscription and service in the army. Immigrants are automatically suspected of having multiple loyalties. Throughout the history of the United States such suspicions and proposals to terminate unwanted immigration have frequently been associated with times of crisis.[14] Thus, it is not surprising that policies of stripping away American citizenship have almost always been connected to military conflicts.

In the United States, the introduction of most bills to revoke citizenship occurred in response to events that generated fear for the existence of the United States as an independent state. The first expatriation laws were introduced during the American Civil War in response to the rising numbers of deserters from the Union army. The Nationality Laws of 1940 were a response to the growing military requirements of the Second World War. The amendment of 1944 dealt with the treatment of Japanese citizens purportedly disloyal to war efforts. In the same manner, the Immigration and Nationality Act of 1952 and the Expatriation Act 1954 were initiated in response to fears generated by the Cold War. The revocation of citizenship is not a random policy that is introduced to sway voters in elections but is connected to militarized conflicts. Citizenship as a social construction has more to do with the actual needs of the state than with a general coherent and stable ideological perception.

On August 19, 1896, Charles W. Eliot, the president of Harvard University, gave an address praising American civilization. In his view, the first principle that established the United States as superior to other national polities was "the advance made in the United States, not in theory only, but in practice, toward the abandonment of war as the means of settling disputes between nations, the substitution of discussion and arbitration, and the avoidance of armaments."[15] Of course, such a declaration would never pass muster today. Not only has the twentieth century demonstrated exactly the opposite, but historical evidence shows that even before that, the United States was constantly engaged in war and its culture was constructed accordingly.[16] As the historical survey of expa-

Table 9.1. Expatriation and Wars in the United States

Conflict	Perceived Enemy	Principle
Civil War	Desertion	Republican
World War I	Immigrants	Ethnic/Liberal
World War II	Japanese Americans	Ethnic
Cold War	Communism	Liberal
War on Terror	Terrorists	Ethnic/Republican

triation policies in the United States shows, it was during (or in relation to) wars that taking away citizenship was initiated. However, it is less clear how military conflict has actually determined or shaped the exact formulation of this policy.

In each of the conflicts that produced legislation to revoke citizenship, the construction of the enemy was different (see Table 9.1). I can describe United States military conflicts using Smith's classification of the three conceptions of citizenship that exist together in the United States: liberalism, "ascriptive inegalitarianism," and republicanism.[17] In the Civil War the perceived danger—desertion—followed republican ideals. In the years prior to the First World War, immigrants were perceived as a threat to the national integrity of the United States. The restrictions imposed on newcomers were justified as both liberal (economic) and ethnic (restriction of immigrants of Asian origin). In the Second World War the definition of the opponent was based on ethnicity (Japanese Americans). And during the Cold War the enemy—Communism—was established in terms of the liberal tradition of citizenship. Nevertheless, during the Vietnam War no new legislation was enacted that denationalized or stripped away American citizenship. It is not that such measures were not considered; rather, the Supreme Court declared invalid the section in the 1940 act that based expatriation upon desertion from the armed forces and the provision that made evading wartime U.S. military service grounds for expatriation.

Immigration and Citizenship Traditions

The study of citizenship consists of many philosophical visions and traditions of understanding the relationship between the individual and the state, and especially between the state and new immigrants. Throughout this study, I have analyzed the various civic ideals of the

United States by looking at these from the perspective of the revocation of citizenship. In the United States, I found that there has been no single political philosophy determining the national order. Defining allegiance, at least in one way, means having an enemy, and while the enemy differed in each conflict, so too did the political position—republican, liberal, or ethnic—that defined the nature of the enemy.

Politicians' acceptance of or ban on multiple loyalties is not determined directly by the ruling political philosophy but by the perception of politics in general. The political ideals that are specifically discussed in the book (liberalism, republicanism, ethno-nationalism, multiculturalism), along with most other perceptions of citizenship (libertarian, civic-republican, left and right communitarian, etc.) are all bound up with national world order and the national logic. Regardless of the scope of rights conferred on individuals by each philosophy, in the end, rights are all limited in one way or another, and the world is divided between those who enjoy those rights and those who don't. Even the liberals who argue that everyone (nationals, citizens, residents, illegal immigrants) should have the same rights almost never apply this rule across national borders. In accordance with this world division, single allegiance is almost mandatory. Since each county is responsible for a limited population and not for people from other political entities, in terms of the national order, it is reasonable to expect that these people be exclusively loyal to their country.

Within the range of possible citizenship regimes (both democratic and non-democratic) some ideologies require more national closure, while others propose individualism. Some thinkers believe in a redesign of borders (such as proponents of the European Union or other regional treaties); some advocate a redistribution of rights (such as rights for guest workers or refugees); and some promote extraterritorial rights (such as rights and protection for nationals/compatriots anywhere in the world). However, truly cosmopolitan citizenship, which grants rights to all people regardless of nationality, religion, residence, and political belief, does not exist. Nevertheless, one policy that might be a sign of coming closer to this post-national ideal is the toleration of multiple national allegiances (and thus the abolition of expatriation policies). While the United States does tolerate dual citizenship, it has not adopted a non-national vision that welcomes dual national loyalty.

To a great extent, the national model would probably have worked if geopolitical borders and migration (voluntary or coerced) were in accordance with this order. In this hypothetical circumstance, the nation-state ideal of a tight fit between the perceived ethnic, religious, cultural, or political borders of nationality and its territorial borders would exist, or at least move in this direction. Common trends of immigration pose a problem for the national imagery, however.[18] Prohibiting dual citizenship is the method a state employs to reinforce the national logic. Toleration of dual citizenship does not stem from a new political philosophy but from the pragmatic needs of states—with regard to immigrants, national security, international relations, or even the management of work in the State Department. These diverse factors work *de facto* to point beyond the national principle; but as they do not directly challenge it, they coexist with it and make it workable.

Political Philosophy and State Action

In order to explain the relationship between the various political philosophies at work in public and official discourse and state action, I develop some of the classical analyses regarding this subject. The traditional Marxist way of thinking about ideology is to show how ideologies involve "false consciousness," a false understanding of the way the world functions. According to Althusser,[19] by contrast, ideology does not reflect the economic base of the world or class position, but "represents" the "imaginary relationship of individuals" to the real world. Different ideologies are different representations of our social and imaginary reality, not representations of the world itself.

Thus, Althusser makes Marx's understanding of the relation between base and superstructure more complex by adding his concept of "ideological state apparatuses." Althusser does not reject the Marxist model. However, he does explore the ways in which ideology is more pervasive (and material) than previously acknowledged. Among the influential state apparatuses are religion, educational systems, family, legal and political systems, trade unions, arts and the media.

Most subjects accept their ideological (subjective) self-constitution and thus there is rarely a need for the state to invoke the repressive state apparatus, which is designed to punish anyone who rejects the dominant ideology. Hegemony is thus less reliant on such repressive state apparatuses, like the police, than it is on the ideological state apparatuses by which ideology is inculcated in all subjects. This point of view was also shared by Weber, according to whom, pure coercion is an extreme case of legitimizing one's authority, whereas domination is usually generated by the subordinate's belief in the system. In Weber's own words "*domination* will thus mean the situation in which the manifested will (*command*) of the ruler or rulers is meant to influence the conduct of one or more others (*the ruled*) and actually does influence it in such a way that their conduct to a socially relevant degree occurs *as if* the ruled had made the content of the command the maxim of their conduct for its very own sake."[20] In our case, it is states through the legal system that install us as subjects, not only of a specific country, but of the national logic that disallows multiple national allegiances. In this sense, the history presented in this book is of the United States as an "instance" of the vicissitudes of a global ideology, ultimately not detachable from it. Voluntary and forced expatriations are state practices that construct (symbolically more than in practice) our vision of the world and its divisions. Even if the number of expatriated citizens does not represent the total population that has dual national loyalty, the provision that allows for expatriation does send a clear message from the administration that multiple allegiances are unacceptable.

While Althusser argued that there is a direct link between the specific state agency and the ideology it introduces, this book shows that the direct connection between ideology and state action is only one of the options for this relationship. The state apparatus can be a representation of state ideology, but it can also be a signifier of grand political shifts rather than being immediately connected to any political philosophy or singular non-contingent act that is only loosely connected to the official ideology. State action can relate to civic ideology in three ways.

First, one can also argue that in the *longue durée*, the actual political institutions and dealings reflect changes in political philosophy. Although they are different in any particular country, three stages, according to my findings, applied to the overall relations between the individual and the state and were consistent with the national imagery. Until the end of the nineteenth century, the common perception of this relationship was as a biological connection. Like the relationship between a child and his or her parents, citizenship could not be transferred or re-moved. Most nations chose to ignore population movement and its con-sequences in favor of the biological perception of perpetual allegiance. In the next phase, during most of the twentieth century, countries tried to enforce unitary loyalty by stripping away the citizenship of those who professed dual nationality. The last stage has been the acceptance of the effect of transnational ties. Increasingly, states have discontinued using revocation policies and have allowed (or at least tolerated) multiple al-legiance. The relationship between the ideology and its practical mani-festation can be very much delayed or prematurely implemented. In the United States, I showed how Hobbes' ideas (like voluntary allegiance or political equality between men and women) were formalized many years after their conception. In the same manner, the republican ideal of citizenship suggested by the American revolutionaries was never fully established. Renunciation fits the modern perception of the state as sig-nifying voluntary consent in political membership. However, the mea-sure that tolerates dual citizenship signifies a post-national ideology, for which the needed institutions have not evolved.

Second, I argue that the practice of expatriation (which is clearly an act of regulating unitary national loyalty) can also be contingent on par-ticular political or practical circumstances. In the United States, expa-triation was usually initiated during military conflicts; it did not reflect any coherent American ideal, but answered a specific need to regulate a part of the population (deserters, women, Communists, immigrants or other minorities), to manage international relations, or to facilitate the work of the State Department.

Third, I have shown that dual citizenship poses a great difficulty for the national logic. Regardless of the particular type of citizenship, multiple allegiances threaten the comprehensiveness of the national ideal. Thus, the United States is still in the liminal stage in which it adheres to the past (but still hegemonic) national logic on one hand, and on the other, is experimenting with new transnational understandings of citizenship. As I have explained, over time, the United States has dropped most of its expatriation measures. At the beginning of the twenty-first century, the facts are that it is almost impossible for a person to lose American citizenship and that millions of Americans have dual citizenship. Despite this, the United States has not changed

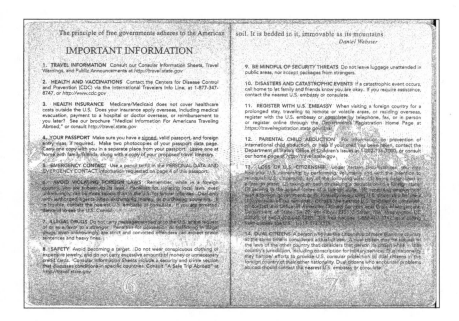

Figure 9.2. Dual Citizenship in the United States Passport

its regulations nor updated the naturalization oath that prohibits dual citizenship. This duality can be observed in the document that is most representative of American citizenship, the United States passport, which explicitly states that holding another nationality might result in loss of American citizenship (Figure 9.2). However, in the next section, it is acknowledged that many Americans do have dual citizenship and that they might encounter problems abroad as a result—the implication being that they would not encounter such problems in the United States (Figure 9.2).

Conclusion

Over the years, several reservations were made to the currently accepted interpretation of the Citizenship Clause of the Fourteenth Amendment especially with respect to the ongoing debates in the United States regarding illegal immigration. In *United States v. Wong Kim Ark* (1898), the United States Supreme Court held that, according to the Fourteenth Amendment, mere birth on U.S. soil automatically confers American citizenship. This interpretation has been the commonly held view until today. But the War on Terror has added security reservations to the concerns about illegal immigration. That is, granting citizenship to any child born within the territory of the United States, especially if his or her parents are illegal or temporary, not only goes against fairness in American immigration policy or American ideals regarding assimilation, but could also potentially constitute a risk to the safety of the state. For many, the case presented at the beginning of the book of Yaser Esam Hamdi, who was an American citizen and a Taliban soldier, illustrates the danger (and irrationality) of the current interpretation of the Constitution.

Here, I would like to connect the arguments discussed throughout the book with one of the claims against the current view of the Citizenship Clause of the Fourteenth Amendment—namely, the claim that this interpretation is incompatible with the political philosophy of the American Founders and that it does not represent the intentions of the drafters of the Fourteenth Amendment. I use the work of John Eastman as representative of this view.[1]

His main argument relies on the specific text used in the Fourteenth Amendment and especially the second part of the clause. The law provides that "All persons born or naturalized in the United States, and subject to the jurisdiction thereof, are citizens of the United States." According to Eastman, the interpretation of the conjunctive part of the sentence has been erroneous. The original meaning invested in the words "and subject to the jurisdiction thereof" was to supplement the provisions by adding the distinction between territorial and political jurisdiction. His contention is that the law-makers of the Fourteenth Amendment wanted to confer citizenship not upon children of foreign nationals, but only upon those who owe complete allegiance to the United States. That is, they found dual national loyalty an undesirable status. For example, Senator Lyman Trumbull, who was one of the main drafters of the Fourteenth Amendment, claimed that "subject to the jurisdiction" of the United States meant "not owing allegiance to anybody else."[2] This interpretation of the law is also consistent with the original American political philosophy that advocated the ideal of citizenship of consent over feudal allegiance. This does not mean that Congress is compelled to deny citizenship based on birthright, but that it has the constitutional authority to do so.

Eastman's reading of the intentions of politicians at the end of the nineteenth century is partially consistent with my analysis of the same period. The common position for most of American history up to the middle of the twentieth century was that dual citizenship should be eradicated. In order to be a "true" American, one ought to have complete and undivided loyalty to the state. While my research has shown that, at that time, an adult had to choose a single allegiance, this study does not directly take a stand in the birthright citizenship debate because voluntary consent was attributed only to adults (and at times only to male adults) rather than to children. Nonetheless, throughout the book, I have also shown that while this approach is still valid as a normative standpoint, it has been completely overturned by the Supreme Court. The current debate over birthright citizenship validates the argument presented here—that even the elite in the United States are still ambivalent regarding the exclusivity of American citizenship.

In this study, I have placed the revocation of citizenship within a sociological framework. That is, I have not only compared the relevant acts of legislation with other legislative measures, but also situated the notion of expatriation within its social, political, economic and historical contexts. I have looked at the legislative history of a law, not to understand another legal text, but to learn about the social atmosphere and cultural meanings that were hegemonic at the time a bill was introduced in Congress. The birthright citizenship debate mentioned above illustrates the difference between the two approaches (social and legal). Eastman was interested in identifying the original intentions of the drafters of the Fourteenth Amendment in order to argue that the current interpretation of the law is flawed. In contrast, in this book I have traced the congressional debates, State Department correspondence, international treaties, and Supreme Court rulings in order to elucidate the common meaning invested in the idea of citizenship at each particular time.

I found that up to the middle of the twentieth century, and to a certain extent even today, the idea of citizenship itself constructs a national world order that is in opposition to dual political membership and thus favors expatriation of those who acquire this status. Bourdieu[3] used the metaphor of a game to describe his notion of the field. According to him, the players are not only trying to win but are constantly struggling over the rules, the value of their capital, the exchange rate, and the boundaries of the game. The key claim of my study is that the loss of citizenship is not determined by its location within the field of citizenship, but derives from the fact that the game is played. The policy of expatriation results from the uncontested assumption that the world is divided into sovereign political entities and that rights are dispensed accordingly.

NOTES

INTRODUCTION

1 For further discussion of these cases, see John Dugard, 1980, "South Africa's 'Independent' Homelands: An Exercise in Denationalization," *Denver Journal of International Law and Policy* 10:11–36; Hannah Arendt, 1979, *The Origins of Totalitarianism* (New York: Harcourt); John C. Torpey, 2000, *The Invention of the Passport: Surveillance, Citizenship, and the State* (Cambridge, UK: Cambridge University Press); Rebecca Kingston, 2005, "The Unmaking of Citizens: Banishment and the Modern Citizenship Regime in France," *Citizenship Studies* 9:23–40; Ralph W. Mathisen, 2006, "Peregrini, Barbari, and Cives Romani: Concepts of Citizenship and the Legal Identity of Barbarians in the Later Roman Empire," *American Historical Review* 11:1011–1040.

2 For example: Rogers M. Smith, 1997, *Civic Ideals: Conflicting Visions of Citizenship in U.S. History* (New Haven, CT: Yale University Press).

3 Jeff Manza and Christopher Uggen, 2006, *Locked Out: Felon Disenfranchisement and American Democracy*, edited by Michael Tonry and Norval Morris (Oxford, UK: Oxford University Press); Rogers M. Smith, 1997, *Civic Ideals: Conflicting Visions of Citizenship in U.S. History* (New Haven, CT: Yale University Press); Chad Alan Goldberg, 2007, *Citizens and Paupers: Relief, Rights and Race from the Freedmen's Bureau to Workfare* (Chicago: University of Chicago Press).

4 Here I follow Elizabeth Cohen in distinguishing between administrative rationality and normative logic of citizenship. Elizabeth F. Cohen, 2009, *Semi-Citizenship in Democratic Politics* (New York: Cambridge University Press). I argue that the revocation of citizenship is much more connected to the former than the latter.

5 Democracy does not prevent any country from executing atrocious or undemocratic practices, but democratic regimes have introduced more obstacles than authoritarian regimes to performing such acts. Democracies are more accountable (to public opinion) for their performance and cannot decide on arbitrary policies that contradict the norms of the general public. Legislation is also limited by legal precedent and constitutional rules.

6 Two important and relevant books, one by Ediberto Román and another by Patrick Weil, have been published during the process of the production of this book. I wish I could have incorporated them to the text as much as they deserve. Ediberto Román, 2013, *Those Damned Immigrants: America's Hysteria over Undocumented Immigration* (New York: New York University Press); Patrick Weil,

2013, *The Sovereign Citizen: Denationalization and the Origins of the American Republic* (Philadelphia: University of Pennsylvania Press).

7 The force of economic circumstance, and flight from war and persecution, challenge this notion of voluntarism and will be discussed below.

CHAPTER 1. REVOKING CITIZENSHIP

1 Engin F. Isin and Patricia K. Wood, 1999, *Citizenship and Identity* (Thousand Oaks, CA: Sage): 4.

2 Rogers Brubaker, 1992, *Citizenship and Nationhood in France and Germany* (Cambridge, MA: Harvard University Press): 178.

3 Christian Joppke and Zeev Roshenhek, 2001, "Ethnic-Priority Immigration in Israel and Germany: Resilience versus Demise" (The Center for Comparative Immigration Studies, University of California San Diego): 5.

4 Among the researchers who ascribe a single kind of citizenship to the different nations are Pamela Johnston Conover, Ivor M. Crewe, and Donald D. Searing, 1991, "The Nature of Citizenship in the United States and Great Britain: Empirical Comments on Theoretical Themes," *Journal of Politics* 53:800–832; David Miller, 2000, *Citizenship and National Identity* (Cambridge, UK: Polity Press); Gérard Noiriel, 1996, *The French Melting Pot: Immigration, Citizenship, and National Identity*, vol. 5 (Minneapolis: University of Minnesota Press); Aihwa Ong, 1999, *Flexible Citizenship: The Cultural Logic of Transnationality* (Durham, NC: Duke University Press); Judith N. Shklar, 1991, *American Citizenship: The Quest for Inclusion* (Cambridge, MA: Harvard University Press); and Michael Walzer, 1992, *What It Means to Be an American* (New York: Marsilio).

5 Examples of these scholars are Seyla Benhabib, 2004, *The Rights of Others: Aliens, Residents and Citizens* (Cambridge, UK: Cambridge University Press); Richard Dagger, 1997, *Civic Virtues: Rights, Citizenship, and Republican Liberalism* (Oxford, UK: Oxford University Press); Thomas Janoski, 1998, *Citizenship and Civil Society: A Framework of Rights and Obligations in Liberal, Traditional, and Social Democratic Regimes* (Cambridge, UK: Cambridge University Press); and Will Kymlicka, 1995, *Multicultural Citizenship: A Liberal Theory of Minority Rights* (Oxford, UK Clarendon).

6 Another important tradition that defines citizenship in addition to the two mentioned by Brubaker (1992) is republicanism—namely, connecting citizenship benefits and rights to active participation in advancing the common good (as understood by the state).

7 Rogers M. Smith, 1997, *Civic Ideals: Conflicting Visions of Citizenship in U.S. History* (New Haven, CT: Yale University Press): 470.

8 Christian Joppke and Zeev Roshenhek, 2001, "Ethnic-Priority Immigration in Israel and Germany: Resilience versus Demise" (The Center for Comparative Immigration Studies, University of California San Diego); Patrick Weil, 2008, *How To Be French: Nationality in the Making since 1789* (Durham, NC: Duke University Press).

9 Rogers Brubaker, 1996, *Nationalism Reframed: Nationhood and the National Question in the New Europe* (New York: Cambridge University Press); Michael Mann, 1987, "Ruling Class Strategies and Citizenship," *Sociology* 21:339–354; Gershon Shafir and Yoav Peled, 2002, *Being Israeli: The Dynamics of Multiple Citizenship* (Cambridge, UK: Cambridge University Press).

10 Michael Walzer, 1983, *Spheres of Justice: A Defense of Pluralism and Equality* (Oxford, UK: Martin Robertson): 62.

11 Pierre Bourdieu and John B. Thompson, 1991, *Language and Symbolic Power* (Cambridge, MA: Harvard University Press): 179.

12 Zygmunt Bauman, 2004, *Wasted Lives: Modernity and Its Outcasts* (Oxford, UK: Polity): 33.

13 Robert R. Alford and Roger Friedland, 1985, *Powers of Theory: Capitalism, the State, and Democracy* (Cambridge, UK: Cambridge University Press).

14 Adriana Kemp, 1999, "The Mirror Language of the Border: Territorial Borders and the Constitution of a National Minority in Israel," *Sociologia Israelit* 3:319–350.

15 Ben Herzog, 2009, "Between Nationalism and Humanitarianism: The Global Discourse on Refugees," *Nations and Nationalism* 15:185–205.

16 Benedict Anderson, 1991, *Imagined Communities* (London: Verso).

17 Ernest Gellner, 1983, *Nations and Nationalism* (Ithaca, NY: Cornell University Press).

18 Hannah Arendt, 1979, *The Origins of Totalitarianism* (New York: Harcourt): 297.

19 John C. Torpey, 2000, *The Invention of the Passport: Surveillance, Citizenship, and the State* (Cambridge, UK: Cambridge University Press).

20 Hannah Arendt, 1994, *Eichmann in Jerusalem: A Report on the Banality of Evil* (New York: Penguin).

21 Giorgio Agamben, 1998, *Homo Sacer: Sovereign Power and Bare Life* (Stanford, CA: Stanford University Press): 131.

22 Zygmunt Bauman, 2004, *Wasted Lives: Modernity and Its Outcasts* (Oxford, UK: Polity).

23 Seyla Benhabib, 2004, *The Rights of Others: Aliens, Residents and Citizens* (Cambridge, UK: Cambridge University Press); David Jacobson, 1996, *Rights Across Borders: Immigration and the Decline of Citizenship* (Baltimore, MD: Johns Hopkins University Press).

24 United States, 2001, *Citizenship Laws of the World* (Washington, DC: U.S Office of Personnel Management, Investigations Service).

25 *Davis v. District Director, INS*, 481 F. Supp, 1178 (D.D.C, 1979).

26 Lawrence Abramson, 1984, "United States Loss of Citizenship Law after Terrazas: Decisions of the Board of Appellate Review," *New York University Journal of International Law and Politics* 16:829–880; Alexander T. Aleinikoff, 1986, "Theories of Loss of Citizenship," *Michigan Law Review* 84:1471–1503; Irving Appleman, 1968, "The Supreme Court on Expatriation: An Historical Review," *Federal Bar Journal* 23:351; Leonard B. Boudin, 1960, "Involuntary Loss of American Nationality," *Harvard Law Review* 73:1510–1531; Edward J.

Cashman, 1967, "Fourteenth Amendment Precludes Involuntary Expatriation," *American University Law Review* 17:86; James Daley, 1958, "Loss of Nationality by Service in a Foreign Army," *Wyoming Law Journal* 14:258; Nora Graham, 2004, "Patriot Act II and Denationalization: An Unconstitutional Attempt to Revive Stripping Americans of Their Citizenship," *Cleveland State Law Review* 52:593; Elwin Griffith, 1988, "Expatriation and the American Citizen," *Howard Law Review* 31:494; Emanuel Gross, 2003, "Defensive Democracy: Is It Possible to Revoke the Citizenship, Deport, or Negate the Civil Rights of a Person Instigating Terrorist Action against His Own State?," *University of Missouri–Kansas City Law Review* 72:51; Henry S. Matteo, 1997, *Denationalization v. "The Right to Have Rights": The Standard of Intent in Citizenship Loss* (Lanham, MD: University Press of America); Amy D. Ronner, 2005, "Denaturalization and Death: What It Means to Preclude the Exercise of Judicial Discretion," *Georgetown Immigration Law Journal* 20:101; David F. Schwartz, 1982, "Citizenship After Afroyim and Bellei: Continuing Controversy," *Hasting Constitutional Law Quarterly* 2:1003.

27 Peter J. Spiro, 2008, *Beyond Citizenship: American Identity after Globalization* (Oxford, UK: Oxford University Press): 5.

28 Michael Walzer, 1983, *Spheres of Justice: A Defense of Pluralism and Equality* (Oxford, UK: Martin Robertson): 62.

29 Of course, not all legislative attempts imply that the proposal is socially acceptable. Fringe groups advance outrageous measures, and it does not mean that they are widely considered legitimate. Nevertheless, the bills discussed here were not introduced by non-mainstream Congress members.

30 Rogers M. Smith, 1997, *Civic Ideals: Conflicting Visions of Citizenship in U.S. History* (New Haven, CT: Yale University Press).

31 Alexander T. Aleinikoff, 1986, "Theories of Loss of Citizenship," *Michigan Law Review* 84:1471–1503.

32 Nancy L. Green, and Francois Weil, 2007, *Citizenship and Those Who Leave: The Politics of Emigration and Expatriation* (Urbana: University of Illinois Press).

33 Alexander T. Aleinikoff, 1986, "Theories of Loss of Citizenship," *Michigan Law Review* 84:1471–1503.

34 Economists use the term "denationalization" to illustrate a similar idea by envisaging denationalization as removing something (an industry, etc.) from state control and transferring it to private ownership.

35 In an attempt to classify all stateless national groups around the world, Minahan reviews 350 groups who identify themselves as national, associated with a particular territory, and deliberately seek self-governance. James Minahan, 2002, *Encyclopedia of the Stateless Nations: Ethnic and Natinal Groups around the World* (London: Greenwood Press). A less strict criterion for a national community would estimate this number as nine thousand.

36 United States, 2001, *Citizenship Laws of the World* (Washington, DC: U.S Office of Personnel Management, Investigations Service).

37 Judith N. Shklar, 1991, *American Citizenship: The Quest for Inclusion* (Cambridge, UK: Harvard University Press): 4.

CHAPTER 2. NATIONAL BEGINNINGS—AMERICAN VERSUS BRITISH CITIZENSHIP

1 I am fully aware that the distinction between subject and citizen is not unequivocal, both historically and analytically. In his *Social Contract* (1762), Rousseau distinguished between citizens as self-governing people and subjects as people bound by the laws of the state. Jean Jacques Rousseau, 1997, "Of the Social Contract or Principles of Political Right," in *Of the Social Contract and Other Political Writings*, edited by Victor Gourevitch (Cambridge, UK: Cambridge University Press). However, even after the U.S. Declaration of Independence, the two terms were used interchangeably; in France's *ancien regime* the term "citizens" was used to refer to the subjects of the king. Analytically, it has to be argued that the conceptual division between subjects and citizens is questionable, as citizenship is a modern technique of constituting, regulating, and governing subjects. See Barbara Cruikshank, 1999, *The Will to Empower: Democratic Citizens and Other Subjects* (Ithaca, NY: Cornell University Press). Nevertheless, in this book I am utilizing this distinction to illustrate the different conceptions of allegiance between the individual and state.

2 Rogers M. Smith, 1997, *Civic Ideals: Conflicting Visions of Citizenship in U.S. History* (New Haven, CT: Yale University Press).

3 Helen Irving, 2004, "Citizenship and Subject-Hood in Twentieth-Century Australia," pp. 9–18 in *From Subjects to Citizens: A Hundred Years of Citizenship in Australia and Canada*, edited by Pierre Boyer, Linda Cardinal, and David Headon (Ottawa: University of Ottawa Press): 9.

4 Rogers M. Smith, 1997, *Civic Ideals: Conflicting Visions of Citizenship in U.S. History* (New Haven, CT: Yale University Press): 42.

5 In the same manner, Casper and Krasner would describe the American perception of citizenship as a constant tension between citizenship as a matter of identity (*Gemeinschaft*) and citizenship as a matter of consent (*Gesellschaft*). Gerhard Casper and Stephen D. Krasner, 2009, "On Citizenship," Review of Peter J. Spiro, *Beyond Citizenship: American Identity after Globalization, American Interest* 4:111–116.

6 Nevertheless, it has been argued that the notion of equal citizenship was partially and temporarily adopted even beforehand in France during the sixteenth century. Charlotte C. Wells, 1995, *Law and Citizenship in Early Modern France* (Baltimore, MD: Johns Hopkins University Press).

7 Peter Shalins, 2004, *Unnaturally French: Foreign Citizens in the Old Regime and After* (Ithaca, NY: Cornell University Press).

8 Rogers Brubaker, 1989a. "The French Revolution and the Invention of Citizenship," *French Politics and the Invention of Citizenship* 7:30–49.

9 Patrick Weil, 2008, *How to Be French: Nationality in the Making since 1789* (Durham, NC: Duke University Press).

10 Peter H. Schuck and Rogers M. Smith, 1985, *Citizenship without Consent: Illegal Aliens in the American Polity* (New Haven, CT: Yale University Press).

11 Rogers Brubaker, 1989b. Introduction, pp. 1–27 in *Immigration and the Politics of Citizenship in Europe and North America*, edited by Rogers Brubaker (Lanham, MD: The German Marshall Fund of the United States; University Press of America): 10.

12 Peter J. Spiro, 1997, "Dual Nationality and the Meaning of Citizenship," *Emory Law Review* 46:1411–1486.

13 David Martin, 2004, "Dual Nationality: TR's 'Self-Evident Absurdity,'" *Chair Lecture*, University of Virginia School of Law.

14 Peter J. Spiro, 1997, "Dual Nationality and the Meaning of Citizenship," *Emory Law Review* 46:1422.

15 John Bassett Moore, 1906, *A Digest of International Law*, vol. 3 (Washington, DC: Government Printing Office).

16 This requirement has now been waived for applicants who suffer a mental disability that renders them unable to understand the oath. Peter J. Spiro, 2008, *Beyond Citizenship: American Identity after Globalization* (Oxford, UK: Oxford University Press): 51.

17 Ibid.

18 For a discussion of the temporal principle in citizenship, see Elizabeth F. Cohen 2011, "Reconsidering U.S. Immigration Reform: The Temporal Principle of Citizenship," *Perspectives on Politics*: 9:575–583.

19 James H. Kettner, 1974, "The Development of American Citizenship in the Revolutionary Era: The Idea of Volitional Allegiance," *American Journal of Legal History* 18:208–242.

20 Gerhard Casper, 2008, "Forswearing Allegiance," *The Maurice and Muriel Fulton Lecture in Legal History*, University of Chicago Law School.

21 Quoted in ibid.

22 Mr. Jefferson, Secretary of State, to Mr. G. Morris, August 16, 1793, quoted in John Bassett Moore, 1906, *A Digest of International Law*, vol. 3 (Washington, DC: Government Printing Office): 562.

23 See Ruth Donner, 1994, *The Regulation of Nationality in International Law* (Irvington-on-Hudson, NY: Transnational Publishers).

24 Edwin Montefiore Borchard, 1928, *The Diplomatic Protection of Citizens Abroad; or, The Law of International Claims* (New York: Banks Law): 674–676.

25 15 *Stat.* 223.

26 This statement was a precursor to his allegation that the United States was one of the last to indicate how its own citizens may elect another nationality. Ulysses S. Grant, State of the Union Address, December 1, 1873.

27 John Bassett Moore, 1906, *A Digest of International Law*, vol. 3 (Washington, DC: Government Printing Office).

28 David Martin, 2004, "Dual Nationality: TR's 'Self-Evident Absurdity,'" *Chair Lecture*, University of Virginia School of Law.

29 Quoted in Gerhard Casper and Stephen D. Krasner, 2009, "On Citizenship," Review of Peter J. Spiro, *Beyond Citizenship: American Identity after Globalization, American Interest* 4:111.

30 Thomas Hobbes, [1651] 1996, *Leviathan*, edited by R. Tuck (Cambridge, UK: Cambridge University Press): bk. 1, chap. 21, p.154.

31 Banishment is a form of punishment imposed on an individual, usually by a country or state, in which the individual is forced to remain outside of that country or state. It is similar to expatriation in that those who lose their citizenship in practice cannot return to their former country. However, in this book I differentiate between the two concepts. Banishment usually signifies an ancient punishment that sought to remove someone from the protection of his or her immediate community. The assumption in using banishment as a punishment is that this protection is restricted to the territory of the community. In contrast, I perceive expatriation as a modern phenomenon connected to the nation-state system in which the status of citizenship extends beyond national borders. The Constitution does not prohibit the employment of banishment; today it is mainly used on Indian reservations.

CHAPTER 3. LEGISLATIVE INITIATIVES

1 This has been done by Alexander T. Aleinikoff, David A. Martin, and Hiroshi Motomura, 2003, *Immigration and Citizenship: Process and Policy* (St. Paul, MN: Thomson/West), and by David Weissbrodt and Laura Danielson, 2005, *Immigration Law and Procedure in a Nutshell* (St. Paul, M–: Thomson/West).

2 United States, 1810, "Resolution Proposing an Amendment to the Constitution of the United States," *Statutes At Large*, vol. 2, Eleventh Congress, Session II, p. 613.

3 Gideon M. Hart, 2010, "The 'Original' Thirteenth Amendment: The Misunderstood Titles of Nobility Amendment," *Marquette Law Review* 94:311–371; Jol A. Silversmith, 1999, "The Missing Thirteenth Amendment: Constitutional Nonsense and Titles of Nobility," *Southern California Interdisciplinary Law Journal* 8:577–612.

4 Patrick Weil, 2008, *How To Be French: Nationality in the Making since 1789* (Durham, NC: Duke University Press).

5 In recent years, right-wing radicals have seized upon the proposed amendment, claiming that it was ratified and suppressed in a wide-ranging conspiracy. They base their accusation on the fact that some textbooks, state compilations of law, and even, on one occasion, a compilation of law published under the auspices of Congress erroneously included TONA as if it had been ratified.

6 J. Harlan, 1967, Dissenting Opinion, *Afroyim v. Rusk*, 387 U.S. 255.

7 A pocket veto is a legislative maneuver in American federal lawmaking and is a process of indirect rejection. The Constitution grants the president ten days to review a measure passed by Congress. If the president has not signed the bill after ten days, it becomes law without his signature. However, if Congress adjourns during the ten-day period, the bill does not become law; this is known as a pocket veto.

8 Nellie Grant, President Ulysses S. Grant's daughter, had her citizenship taken
   away after she married a British subject and moved to England in the late
   nineteenth century. The Bancroft Treaty with Great Britain stated that Americans
   who naturalize within the British dominions shall be treated as British subjects.
   After the death of her husband, she returned to the United States and had her
   citizenship reinstated. Frederick Van Dyne, 1904, *Citizenship of the United State*
   (Rochester, NY: Lawyers' Co-operative). See Chapter 4 for a discussion of the
   Bancroft treaties.

9 Candice Lewis Bredbenner, 1998, *A Nationality of Her Own: Women, Marriage,
   and the Law of Citizenship* (Berkeley: University of California Press).

10 Hobbes' constructivist approach to gender relations can be interpreted in
   opposing ways. Carole Pateman argues that Hobbes' social contract reinforced
   male dominance by reconfirming modern patriarchy. Conversely, Joanne H.
   Wright claims that Hobbes' writings can be described as provocative and
   important to the theorization of gender relations. Carole Pateman, 1998, *The
   Sexual Contract* (Cambridge, UK: Polity); Joanne H. Wright, 2002, "Going against
   the Grain: Hobbes's Case for Original Maternal Dominion," *Journal of Women's
   History* 14:123–155.

11 Thomas Hobbes, [1651] 1996, *Leviathan*, edited by R. Tuck (Cambridge, UK:
   Cambridge University Press): bk. 1, chap. 20, p.139.

12 Nancy F. Cott, 1998, "Marriage and Women's Citizenship in the United States,
   1830–1934," *American Historical Review* 103:1440–1474.

13 HR 15442, passed on June 29, 1906, established the Bureau of Immigration and
   Naturalization (INS) to provide, for the first time, a uniform naturalization
   process throughout the United States. This bill stated that all immigrants had to
   declare that they "renounce absolutely and forever all allegiance and fidelity to
   any foreign prince, potentate, state, or sovereignty," but did not include measures
   for denaturalization.

14 Ann Marie Nicolosi, 2001, "'We Do Not Want Our Girls to Marry Foreigners':
   Gender, Race, and American Citizenship," *National Women's Studies Association
   Journal* 13: 8.

15 An Act to Revise and Codify the Nationality Laws of the United States into a
   Comprehensive Nationality Code/ Nationality Act of 1940 (HR 9980), 1940,
   Congressional Record, 76th Congress, Session III, pp. 11940, 11943, and 11949.

16 For instance, Alexander T. Aleinikoff, 1986, "Theories of Loss of Citizenship,"
   Michigan Law Review 84:1471–1503. See also David Weissbrodt and Laura
   Danielson, 2005, *Immigration Law and Procedure in a Nutshell* (St. Paul, MN:
   Thomson/West).

17 Donald E. Collins, 1985, *Native American Aliens: Disloyalty and the Renunciation
   of Citizenship by Japanese Americans during World War II* (Westport, CT:
   Greenwood).

18 Charles A. Halleck and Leroy J. Johnson, 1944, An Act to Provide for Loss of
   United States Nationality under Certain Circumstances (HR 4103), 1944,

Congressional Record, 78th Congress, Session II, pp. 1779; Thomas Rolph, ibid., pp. 1780.

19 One of the ironic twists of history is that in spring of 1945, the 522nd Field Artillery Battalion, which was composed of young Japanese American men (many of whom had families interned in the relocation camps in the United States), was among the forces that liberated the Dachau concentration camp in Germany. Linda K. Menton, 1994, "Research Report: Nisei Soldiers at Dachau, Spring 1945," *Holocaust and Genocide Studies* 8:258–27.

20 Richard Harless, 1944, An Act to Provide for Loss of United States Nationality under Certain Circumstances (HR 4103), 1944, *Congressional Record*, 78th Congress, Session II, pp. 1787.

21 Alicia J. Campi, 2004, *The McCarran-Walter Act: A Contradictory Legacy on Race, Quotas, and Ideology* (Washington, DC: American Immigration Law Foundation).

22 The Alien Registration Act, or Smith Act, of 1940 made it a criminal offense for anyone to "knowingly or willfully advocate, abet, advise or teach the [. . .] desirability or propriety of overthrowing the Government of the United States or of any State by force or violence, or for anyone to organize any association which teaches, advises or encourages such an overthrow, or for anyone to become a member of or to affiliate with any such association."

23 Dwight D. Eisenhower, 1954, State of the Union address, pp. 6–23 in *Public Papers of the Presidents of the United States* (Washington, DC: Government Printing Office).

24 The purpose of considering bills under suspension is to dispose of noncontroversial measures expeditiously. A motion to suspend the rules requires a vote of two-thirds of the members present and voting, and no amendments are in order unless submitted with the bill by its manager at the time the motion to suspend the rules is offered. Stanley Bach, 1990, "Suspension of the Rules, the Order of Business, and the Development of Congressional Procedure," *Legislative Studies Quarterly* 15:49–63.

25 Patrick MaCarran, 1954, An Act to Amend the Immigration and Nationality Act To Provide for the Loss of Nationality of Persons Convicted of Certain Crimes/ Expatriation Act of 1954 (HR 7130)," *Congressional Record*, 83rd Congress, Session II, p. 14983.

26 Nonetheless, the court did not always oppose denationalization whenever it was challenged.

27 Rogers M. Smith, 1997, *Civic Ideals: Conflicting Visions of Citizenship in U.S. History* (New Haven, CT: Yale University Press): 6.

28 As mentioned above, the latter could also be seen as undermining the logic of singular national allegiance, not because of the Soviet Union, but because of the commitments implied by "workers of the world unite."

29 Carl Schmitt, 1985, *Political Theology: Four Chapters on the Concept of Sovereignty* (Cambridge, MA: MIT Press).

30 Carl Schmitt, 1976, *The Concept of the Political* (New Brunswick, NJ: Rutgers University Press).

31 Rogers Brubaker, 1996, *Nationalism Reframed: Nationhood and the National Question in the New Europe* (New York: Cambridge University Press): 15.

CHAPTER 4. INTERNATIONAL RELATIONS

1 Although the Bancroft Treaties usually designate bilateral agreements between the United States and a foreign country, the Inter-American Convention of 1906 follows similar principles and can be regarded as another Bancroft Treaty. The Inter-American Convention was signed by the United States, Ecuador, Paraguay, Bolivia, Colombia, Honduras, Panama, Cuba, Peru, Salvador, Costa Rica, Mexico, Guatemala, Uruguay, Argentina, Nicaragua, Brazil, and Chile and declared that naturalized citizens who again take up residence in their country of origin would lose their naturalized citizenship.

2 Alfred M. Boll, 2007, *Multiple Nationality and International Law* (Leiden, NDL: Martinus Nijhoff).

3 Peter Kivisto and Thomas Faist, 2007, *Citizenship: Discourse, Theory, and Transnational Prospects* (Malden, MA: Blackwell).

4 Rey Koslowski, 2002, "Challenges of International Cooperation in a World of Increasing Dual Citizenship," pp. 157–182 in *Rights and Duties of Dual Nationals: Evolution and Prospects*, edited by David Martin and Kay Hailbronner (Leiden, NDL: Brill Academic Publishers).

5 J. Douglas, 1964, Opinion of the Court, *Schneider v. Rusk*, 377 U.S, 163.

6 Michael Walter, 1978, "The Bancroft Conventions: Second-Class Citizenship for Naturalized Americans," *International Lawyer* 12:825–833.

7 The Selective Service Act, or Selective Draft Act (P.L. 65–12, 40 Stat. 76), was passed by the Congress of the United States on May 18, 1917. At the time of the First World War, the U.S. Army was tiny compared with the mobilized armies of the European powers. Therefore, the act authorized the federal government to raise a national army numbering in the hundreds of thousands with which to fight a modern war. The act was canceled with the end of the war on November, 1918. Mark E. Grotelueschen, 2007, *The AEF Way of War: The American Army and Combat in World War I* (Cambridge, UK: Cambridge University Press).

8 Formation of blocs can be seen as a refinement of the national world order. For example, the boundaries in the European Community, allowing ease of movement and work, as well as a common currency, were described as the consolidation of new boundaries. Michael Mann, 1993, "Nation-States in Europe and Other Continents: Diversifying, Developing, Not Dying," *Daedalus* 122: 115–140.

9 *Title 8, Aliens and Citizenship*, 1940, §349(a)(8), pp.

10 12 *Bevans* 1968, 381.

11 Frank Billings Kellogg (1856–1937) was the United States secretary of state in the
    cabinet of President Calvin Coolidge (1925–1929). He coauthored the Kellogg-
    Briand Pact, the treaty intended to provide for "the renunciation of war as an
    instrument of national policy" (46 *Stat.* 2343), for which he was awarded
    the Nobel Peace Prize in 1929. Lewis Ethan Ellis, 1961, *Frank B. Kellogg and
    American Foreign Relations, 1925–1929* (New Brunswick, NJ: Rutgers University
    Press).

12 Frank B. Kellogg, 1928, "Proposals to European Countries for Agreements and
    Treaties Regarding Naturalization, Dual nationality, and Military Service," *Foreign
    Relations of the United States*, vol. 1, p. 496.

13 House of Representatives, 1928, *Hearing before the Committee on Foreign Affairs
    on HJR 195 and HJR 268*, 17th Congress, Session I, Washington, DC: Government
    Printing Office.

14 "Communication of Negotiations with Certain European Countries for
    Agreements and Treaties Regarding Naturalization, Dual Nationality, and
    Military Service," 1929, *Foreign Relations*, vol. 1, pp. 439–486.

15 Naturalization Treaty—Albania (1932), 49 *Stat.* 3241–3244; Lithuania—Military
    Service (1937), 53 *Stat.* 1569–1572; Naturalization Treaty—Bulgaria (1923), 5
    Bevans, pp. 1083–1085.

16 League of Nations, April 13, 1930, *Convention on Certain Questions Relating to the
    Conflict of Nationality Law*, League of Nations, Treaty Series, vol. 179, p. 89–114,
    no. 4137, available at http://www.unhcr.org/refworld/docid/3ae6b3b00.html.

17 Ibid., 93.

18 Peter Kivisto and Thomas Faist, 2007, *Citizenship: Discourse, Theory, and
    Transnational Prospects* (Malden, MA: Blackwell).

19 Manley O. Hudson, 1930, "The First Conference for the Codification of
    International Law," *The American Journal of International Law* 24:447–466;
    Richard W. Flournoy, Jr., 1930, "Nationality Convention, Protocols and
    Recommendations Adopted by the First Conference on the Codification of
    International Law," *American Journal of International Law* 24:467–485; Hunter
    Miller, 1930, "The Hague Codification Conference," *American Journal of
    International Law* 24:674–693.

20 Ruth Donner, 1994, *The Regulation of Nationality in International Law* (Irvington-
    on-Hudson, NY: Transnational).

21 5 *Bevans* 1968: 150.

22 60 *Stat.* 341.

23 U.N. General Assembly, August 30, 1961, *Convention on the Reduction of
    Statelessness*, United Nations, Treaty Series, vol. 989, p. 175, available at http://
    www.unhcr.org/refworld/docid/3ae6b39620.html.

24 Ibid.

25 Linda K. Kerber, 2007, "Presidential Address: The Stateless as the Citizen's Other:
    A View from the United States," *American Historical Review* 112:1–34.

26 Council of Europe, May 6, 1963, *Convention on Reduction of Cases of Multiple Nationality and Military Obligations in Cases of Multiple Nationality*, European Treaty Series 43, available at http://www.unhcr.org/refworld/docid/3ae6b37814. html.

27 Tomas Hammar, 1985, "Dual Citizenship and Political Integration," *International Migration Review* 19:438–450.

28 Council of Europe, November 24, 1977, *Protocol Amending the Convention on the Reduction of Cases of Multiple Nationality and Military Obligations in Cases of Multiple Nationality*, 24 November 1977, European Treaty Series 95, available at http://www.unhcr.org/refworld/docid/3ae6b37a18.html; Council of Europe, November 24, 1977, *Additional Protocol to the Convention on the Reduction of Cases of Multiple Nationality and Military Obligations in Cases of Multiple Nationality*, European Treaty Series 96, available at http://www.unhcr.org/ refworld/docid/3ae6b37a4.html.

29 Council of Europe, February 2, 1993, *Second Protocol Amending the Convention on the Reduction of Cases of Multiple Nationality and Military Obligations in Cases of Multiple Nationality*, European Treaty Series 149, available at http://www.unhcr. org/refworld/docid/3ae6b37f20.html.

30 Council of Europe, November 6, 1997, *European Convention on Nationality*, European Treaty Series 166, available at http://www.unhcr.org/refworld/ docid/3ae6b36618.html.

31 Jeffrey T. Checkel, 2001, "The Europeanization of Citizenship?" pp. 180–197 in *Transforming Europe: Europeanization and Domestic Change*, edited by Maria Green Cowles, James Caporaso, and Thomas Risse (Ithaca, NY: Cornell University Press).

32 Peter J. Spiro, 2008, *Beyond Citizenship: American Identity after Globalization* (Oxford, UK: Oxford University Press): 72.

33 Peter Kivisto and Thomas Faist, 2007, *Citizenship: Discourse, Theory, and Transnational Prospects* (Malden, MA: Blackwell).

34 Peter J. Spiro, 2002a, "Embracing Dual Nationality," pp. 19–33 in *Dual Nationality, Social Rights, and Federal Citizenship in the U.S. and Europe: The Reinvention of Citizenship*, edited by Randall Hansen and Patrick Weil (New York: Berghahn).

CHAPTER 5. CONSULAR DILEMMAS

1 Quoted in Francis Wharton, 1886, *A Digest of the International Law of the United States: Taken from Documents Issued by Presidents and Secretaries of State, and from Decisions of Federal Courts and Opinions of Attorneys-General* (Washington, DC: Government Printing Office): 446.

2 Peter J. Spiro, 2002a, "Embracing Dual Nationality," pp. 19–33 in *Dual Nationality, Social Rights, and Federal Citizenship in the U.S. and Europe: The Reinvention of Citizenship*, edited by Randall Hansen and Patrick Weil (New York: Berghahn).

3 John Hay, 1899, Circulars, Passports for Persons Residing or Sojourning Abroad, *Foreign Relations of the United States*, p. 2.

4 Thomas F. Bayard, 1887, Correspondence Regarding American Citizens in Switzerland, *Foreign Relations of the United States*, p. 1074.

5 Ibid.

6 John Hay, 1899, Circulars, Passports for Persons Residing or Sojourning Abroad, *Foreign Relations of the United States*, p. 2.

7 Edward W. Said, 1978, *Orientalism* (New York: Vintage).

8 John Hay, 1899, Circulars, Passports for Persons Residing or Sojourning Abroad, 1899, *Foreign Relations of the United States*, p. 3.

9 James Perkins, 1907, An Act in Reference to the Expatriation of Citizens and Their Protection Abroad / 1907 Expatriation Act (HR 24122), *Congressional Record*, 59th Congress, Session II, p. 1464.

10 In 1882 Congress passed the Chinese Exclusion Act, barring immigration for ten years; the Geary Act extended the act for another ten years in 1892; and by the Extension Act of 1904, the act was made permanent. Only since the 1940s, when the United States and China became allies during the Second World War, did the situation for Chinese Americans begin to improve, as restrictions on entry into the country, naturalization, and mixed marriage were eased. In 1943, Chinese immigration to the United States was once again permitted, but large-scale Chinese immigration did not take place until 1965 when the Immigration and Nationality Act of 1965 lifted national origin quotas.

11 Philander C. Knox, 1911, "Expatriation," *Foreign Relations of the United States*, p. 1.

CHAPTER 6. SUPREME COURT RULINGS

1 Alexander T. Aleinikoff, 1986, "Theories of Loss of Citizenship," *Michigan Law Review* 84: 1471–1503.

2 Patrick Weil, 2013. *The Sovereign Citizen: Denationalization and the Origins of the American Republic* (Philadelphia: University of Pennsylvania Press).

3 *Trop v. Dulles*, 356 U.S. 86 (1958).

4 Chief Justice Earl Warren, 1958, *Trop v. Dulles* 356 U.S. 86.

5 Bernard Schwartz, 1996, *The Warren Court: A Retrospective* (Oxford, UK: Oxford University Press); Morton J. Horwitz, 1998, *The Warren Court and the Pursuit of Justice: A Critical Issue* (New York: Hill and Wang).

6 *Brown v. Board of Education*, 347 U.S. 483 (1954).

7 *Baker v. Carr*, 369 U.S, 186 (1962).

8 *Miranda v. Arizona*, 384 U.S. 436 (1966).

9 *Griswold v. Connecticut*, 381 U.S. 479 (1965).

10 *Afroyim v. Rusk*, 387 U.S. 255 (1967).

11 *Vance v. Terrazas*, 444 U.S. 252 (1980).

12 In contrast to the language of the law and the assumptions of some of its current interpreters (judges, members of Congress, lawyers, and academic scholars), revocation of citizenship in the United States was usually initiated and practiced as a punitive measure. Title 8, chapter 12, subchapter III, part III of the U.S. Code,

which details the current laws regarding loss of nationality and expatriation, clearly states that expatriation is a voluntary action on the part of a citizen rather than a penalty for insubordination imposed by the government: "A person who is a national of the United States whether by birth or naturalization, shall lose his nationality by voluntarily performing any of the following acts with the intention of relinquishing United States nationality."

13 *Perez v. Brownell* 356 U.S. 44 (1958).

14 Alexander T. Aleinikoff, David A. Martin, and Hiroshi Motomura, 2003, *Immigration and Citizenship: Process and Policy* (St. Paul, MN: Thomson/West).

15 Ibid.

16 *Rogers v. Bellei*, 401 U.S. 819 (1971).

17 The two cases are different in relation to the Constitution. Afroyim was naturalized in the United States; Bellei (having been born abroad as a citizen) was not a Fourteenth Amendment first-sentence citizen. However, they both questioned whether Congress has the power to take away citizenship in a particular situation.

18 Act of October 10, 1978, Pub.L. 95–432, 92 *Stat.* 1046.

19 *Vance v. Terrazas*, 444 U.S. 252 (1980).

20 Steven S. Goodman, 1988, "Protecting Citizenship: Strengthening the Intent Requirement in Expatriation Proceedings," *George Washington Law Review* 56:341–372.

21 It is commonly accepted that actions have greater validity than words. Such understandings were expressed in the Bible and continue to be influential today. For example, John wrote, "But whoever has the world's goods, and beholds his brother in need and closes his heart against him, how does the love of God abide in him? Little children, let us not love with word or with tongue, but in deed and truth" (1 John 3:17, 18). A secular perspective emerges in John Locke's statement that "I have always thought the actions of men the best interpreters of their thoughts" or in Benjamin Franklin's observation that "Well done is better than well said."

22 Public Law 414, 1952, 66 Stat. 268.

23 Alexander T. Aleinikoff, 1986, "Theories of Loss of Citizenship," *Michigan Law Review* 84: 1471–1503.

24 *Afroyim v. Rusk*, 387 U.S. 255 (1967).

25 *Vance v. Terrazas*, 444 U.S. 252 (1980).

26 Alexander T. Aleinikoff, 1986, "Theories of Loss of Citizenship," *Michigan Law Review* 84:1499.

27 Yoav Peled, 1992, "Ethnic Democracy and the Legal Construction of Citizenship: Arab Citizens of the Jewish State," *American Political Science Review* 86:432.

28 Given that he wanted to be an Israeli parliamentarian, his renunciation was not altogether uncoerced. Perhaps the fact that he wanted to be a law maker in another country was a particularly sharp and public challenge to the notion of unitary loyalty.

29 *Vance v. Tarrazas*, 444 U.S. 252 (1980).

30 A report by Mr. Mazzoli of the Committee on the Judiciary on the Immigration and Nationality Amendments of 1986, p. 23.

31 Joan Clark, 1986, *Hearing before the Subcommittee on Immigration, Refugees and International Law of the Committee on the Judiciary*, July 22, 99th Congress, 2nd Session (Washington, DC: Government Printing Office): 151.

32 *Rogers v. Bellei*, 401 U.S. 815 (1971).

CHAPTER 7. THE BOARD OF APPELLATE REVIEW

1 Lawrence Abramson, 1984, "United States Loss of Citizenship Law after Terrazas: Decisions of the Board of Appellate Review," *New York University Journal of International Law and Politics* 16:829–880.

2 Ibid.; Alan G. James, 1986, "The Board of Appellate Review of the Department of State: The Right to Appellate Review of Administrative Determinations of Loss of Nationality," *San Diego Law Review* 23:261–326.

3 I was able to find complete records of appeals only from 1982 to 1996. Official statistics on expatriation were released only for the years 1949–1985. In this section, I have chosen to include the years 1982–1985 alone, as only in those years do I have full data on both the overall expatriation rate and appeals regarding the loss of citizenship. About 6 percent of the citizens who lost their citizenship appealed to the Board of Appellate Review to reconsider their cases.

4 John Mollenhauer, 1985, *Decisions of the Board of Appellate Review*, vol. 10, p. 189.

5 Warren E. Hewitt, 1985, *Decisions of the Board of Appellate Review*, vol. 10, p. 198.

6 The appellants came from forty-eight countries from around the world, although most were from the Western Hemisphere. Half the 459 known cases came from Canada and Mexico. Lower down on the list were Australia, Germany, Israel, the Philippines, the United Kingdom, and Venezuela, which had between ten and forty appellants each. The rest of the countries had five or fewer representatives in the board's cases. Those countries were Argentina, Austria, Belgium, Brazil, Chile, Costa Rica, Cyprus, Denmark, Egypt, El Salvador, Finland, France, Greece, Guatemala, Guyana, Hong Kong, Iceland, India, Iraq, Italy, Jamaica, Japan, Korea, Liberia, Malta, Morocco, Netherlands, New Zealand, Nicaragua, Nigeria, Norway, Panama, Peru, Poland, Rhodesia, Saudi Arabia, Spain, Sweden, Switzerland, and Uganda.

7 Section 19(1)(b) of Canadian Citizenship Regulation P.C, 1968–1703 of August 28, 1968. The renunciation clause was deleted from the Canadian oath on April 30, 1973. The United States still has such a clause in its naturalization oath.

8 Joseph B. Glass, 2002, *From New Zion to Old Zion: American Jewish Immigration and Settlement in Palestine, 1917–1939* (Detroit, MI: Wayne State University Press).

9 Alan G. James, Edward G. Misey, George Taft, 1985, *Decisions of the Board of Appellate Review*. Vol. 11, p. 149.

10 Charles Stuart Kennedy, 1994, "Interview with Alan G. James," Foreign Affairs Oral History Collection of the Association for Diplomatic Studies and Training, Washington, DC.

11 Alan G. James, Mary E. Hoinkes, James G. Sampas, 1985, *Decisions of the Board of Appellate Review*, vol. 11, p. 174.

12 Ibid., p. 175

13 Alan G. James, 1991, "Cult-Induced Renunciation of United States Citizenship: The Involuntary Expatriation of Black Hebrews," *San Diego Law Review* 25:645–670.

14 Elizabeth F. Cohen, 2009, *Semi-Citizenship in Democratic Politics* (New York: Cambridge University Press).

15 Margaret S. Pickering, Sally J. Cummins, and David P. Stewart, 2002, "Digest of United States Practice in International Law, 1989–1990" (Washington, DC: International Law Institute): 4.

16 Alan G. James, 1990, "Expatriation in the United States: Precepts and Practice Today and Yesterday," *San Diego Law Review* 27:853–905.

17 Code of Federal Regulations, Title 22: Foreign Relations, Part 50—Nationality Procedures, Subpart C—Loss of Nationality, § 50.40 Certification of loss of U.S. nationality.

CHAPTER 8. THE WAR ON TERROR

1 Henry Ansgar Kelly, 1991, "Dual Nationality, the Myth of Election, and a Kinder, Gentler State Department," *University of Miami Inter-American Law Review* 23.

2 Peter J. Spiro, 2002b. "Political Rights and Dual Nationality," pp. 135–152 in *Rights and Duties of Dual Nationals: Evolution and Prospects*, edited by David Martin and Kay Hailbronner (Leiden, NLD: Brill):135.

3 David Martin, 1999, "New Rules on Dual Nationality for a Democratizing Globe: Between Rejection and Embrace," *Georgetown Immigration Law Journal* 14:1–34.

4 Joachim K. Blatter, Sterfeanie Erdmann, and Katja Schwanke, 2009, *Acceptance of Dual Citizenship: Empirical Data and Political Contexts* (Lucerne: Institute of Political Science; University of Lucerne).

5 Alfred M. Boll, 2007, *Multiple Nationality and International Law* (Leiden, NDL: Martinus Nijhoff Publishers); Isabelle Chopin, 2006, "Administrative Practices in the Acquisition of Nationality," pp. 221–268 in *Acquisition and Loss of Nationality: Policies and Trends in 15 European Countires*, vol. 1: *Comparative Analyses*, edited by Rainer Baubock, Eva Ersboll, Kees Groenendijk, and Harald Waldrauch (Amsterdam: Amsterdam University Press); Marc Moje Howard, 2005, "Variation in Dual Citizenship in the Countries of the E.U.," *International Migration Review* 39:697–720; Michael Jones-Cerrera, 2001, "Under Two Flags: Dual Nationality in Latin America and Its Consequences for Naturalization in the United States," *International Migration Review* 35:997–1029; Stanley A. Renshon, 2005, *The 50% American: Immigration and National Identity in an Age of Terror* (Washington, DC: Georgetown University Press); Tanja B. Sejersen, 2008, "'I Vow to Thee My Country'—The Expansion of Dual Citizenship in the 21st Century," *International Migration Review* 42:523–549; United States, 2001, *Citizenship Laws of the World* (Washington, DC: U.S Office of Personnel Management, Investigations Service);

Jeffrey K. Staton, Robert Jackson, and Damarys Canache, 2007, "Costly Citizenship? Dual Nationality Institutions, Naturalization, and Political Connectedness," *Social Science Research Network*. Available at http://ssrn.com/abstract=995569; Patrick Weil, 2001, "Access to Citizenship: A Comparison of Twenty-Five Nationality Laws," pp. 17–35 in *Citizenship Today: Global Perspectives and Practices*, edited by Thomas A. Aleinikoff and Douglas Klusmeyer (Washington, DC: Brookings Institution).

6   Peter J. Spiro, 2008, *Beyond Citizenship: American Identity after Globalization* (Oxford; New York: Oxford University Press): 61.

7   David Martin, 1999, "New Rules on Dual Nationality for a Democratizing Globe: Between Rejection and Embrace," *Georgetown Immigration Law Journal* 14:1–34.

8   Nora Graham, 2004, "Patriot Act II and Denationalization: An Unconstitutional Attempt to Revive Stripping Americans of Their Citizenship," *Cleveland State Law Review* 52:593.

9   Draft of *Domestic Security Enhancement Act of 2003*, section-by-section analysis, January 9, 2003:78–79 (emphasis in origin). Available at http://www.pbs.org/now/politics/patriot2-hi.pdf.

10 Timothy Scahill, 2006, "The Domestic Security Enhancement Act of 2003: A Glimpse into a Post–Patriot Act Approach to Combating Domestic Terrorism," *CR: The New Centennial Review* 6:69–94.

11 *United States v. Schiffer*, 831 F. Supp, 1166 (1993).

12 Charles Lewis and Adam Mayle, 2003, "Justice Department Drafts Sweeping Expansion of Anti-Terrorism Act," Center for Public Integrity. Available at http://www.publicintegrity.org/2003/02/07/3159/justice-dept-drafts-sweeping-expansion-anti-terrorism-act.

13 *Yaser Esam Hamdi v. Donald Rumsfeld*, Settlement Agreement, September 17, 2004: 1–2. Available at http://news.findlaw.com/hdocs/docs/hamdi/91704stlagrmnt.html.

14 Abbe L. Dienstag, 1982, "*Fedorenko v. United States*: War Crimes, the Defense of Duress, and American Nationality Law," *Columbia Law Review* 82:120–183.

15 *United States v. Kumpf*, 438 U.S. 785 (2006).

16 Amy D. Ronner, 2005, "Denaturalization and Death: What It Means to Preclude the Exercise of Judicial Discretion," *Georgetown Immigration Law Journal* 20:101–132.

17 Ibid., p. 117.

18 See also Shai Lavi, 2011, "Citizenship Revocation as Punishment: On the Modern Duties of Citizens and Their Criminal Breach," *University of Toronto Law Journal* 61:783–810.

19 Joanne Mariner, 2004, "Patriot II's Attack on Citizenship," CNN.com.

20 Lieberman Joseph, 2010, Terrorist Expatriation Act (S. 3327), *Congressional Record*, 111th Congress, Session II, p. 2.

21 Interview with Joseph Lieberman, 2010. Available at http://www.foxnews.com/story/2010/05/06/lieberman-aims-legislation-at-terrorists/.

22 Stanley A. Renshon, 2005, *The 50% American: Immigration and National Identity in an Age of Terror* (Washington, DC: Georgetown University Press).

23 Nathan Glazer, 2002, "Dual Citizenship as a Challenge to Sovereignty," pp. 33–54 in *Sovereignty under Challenge: How Governments Respond*, edited by John D. Montgomery and Nathan Glazer (New Brunswick, NJ: Transaction Publishers): 52.

CHAPTER 9. DUAL CITIZENSHIP AND THE REVOCATION OF CITIZENSHIP

1 Hannah Arendt, 1979, *The Origins of Totalitarianism* (New York: Harcourt); John Dugard, 1980, "South Africa's 'Independent' Homelands: An Exercise in Denationalization," *Denver Journal of International Law and Policy* 10:11–36; Rebecca Kingston, 2005, "The Unmaking of Citizens: Banishment and the Modern Citizenship Regime in France," *Citizenship Studies* 9:23–40; Ralph W. Mathisen, 2006, "Peregrini, Barbari, and Cives Romani: Concepts of Citizenship and the Legal Identity of Barbarians in the Later Roman Empire," *American Historical Review* 11:1011–1040; John C. Torpey, 2000, *The Invention of the Passport: Surveillance, Citizenship, and the State* (Cambridge, UK: Cambridge University Press).

2 Irene Bloemraad, 2007, "Much Ado about Nothing? The Contours of Dual Citizenship in the United States and Canada," pp. 159–186 in *Dual Citizenship in Global Perspective: From Unitary to Multiple Citizenship*, edited by Thomas Faist, and Peter Kivisto (New York: Palgrave Macmillan).

3 Since the 1980s both liberal and conservative governments have signaled their desire to enact amendments to the Citizenship Act. Those attempts include producing discussion papers, initiating committees, and even introducing bills in the Canadian Parliament (Bill C-63, C-16, and C-18). However, up to the present, none of those attempts has actually materialized into a revision of the 1977 Citizenship Act.

4 Peter Nyers, 2009, *Securitization of Citizenship* (New York: Routledge).

5 Another reason for the revocation of citizenship would be the annulment process. This measure gives the government a new power to expatriate naturalized citizens in the first five years after the original citizenship decision. This annulment mechanism would in effect create a status of citizens on probation.

6 In addition, Canada had also assisted in evacuating 699 foreign nationals from thirty-two countries.

7 Peter Nyers, 2010, "Dueling Designs: The Politics of Rescuing Dual Citizens," *Citizenship Studies* 14:47–60.

8 The requirement of the oath has recently been waived for applicants who suffer a mental disability. Peter J. Spiro, 2008, *Beyond Citizenship: American Identity after Globalization* (Oxford, UK: Oxford University Press). Moreover, the oath can be

modified if the applicant provides enough evidence that his or her religious training and beliefs prevent reciting certain language contained in the oath of allegiance. However, the renunciation requirement cannot be waived. Karen Scherner-Kim, 2000, "The Role of the Oath of Renunciation in Current U.S. Nationality Policy—to Enforce, to Omit, or Maybe to Change," *Georgetown Law Journal* 88:329–380.

9   Gerald L. Neuman, 1994, "Justifying U.S. Naturalization Policies," *Immigration and Nationality Law Review* 16:83–126.

10   Peter J. Spiro, 1997, "Dual Nationality and the Meaning of Citizenship," *Emory Law Review* 46:1411–1486; Peter J. Spiro, 1998, "Questioning Barriers to Naturalization," *Georgetown Immigration Law Journal* 13:479–519.

11   Alexander T. Aleinikoff, 1998, *Between Principles and Politics: The Direction of U.S. Citizenship Policy* (Washington, DC: Carnegie Endowment for International Peace); Peter H. Schuck, 1998, *Citizens, Strangers, and In-Betweens: Essays on Immigration and Citizenship* (Boulder, CO: Westview).

12   Karen Scherner-Kim, 2000, "The Role of the Oath of Renunciation in Current U.S. Nationality Policy—To Enforce, To Omit, or Maybe To Change," *Georgetown Law Journal* 88:329–380.

13   Elliot Cohen, 1985, *Citizens and Soldiers: The Dilemmas of Military Service* (Ithaca, NY: Cornell University Press); Deborah Cowen and Emily Gilbert, 2008, *War, Citizenship, Territory* (New York: Routledge); Chad Alan Goldberg, 2007, *Citizens and Paupers: Relief, Rights and Race from the Freedmen's Bureau to Workfare* (Chicago: University of Chicago Press); Michael Mann, 1988, *States, War and Capitalism: Studies in Political Sociology* (Oxford, UK: Basil Blackwell); Max Weber, 1978, *Economy and Society: An Outline of Interpretive Sociology* (Berkeley: University of California Press).

14   Ediberto Román, 2006, "The Citizenship Dialectic," *Georgetown Immigration Law Journal* 20: 557–610.

15   Charles William Eliot, 1897, *American Contribution to Civilization and Other Essays and Addresses* (New York: The Century Co.): 2.

16   Fred Anderson and Andrew Cayton, 2005, *The Dominion of War: Empire and Liberty in North America, 1500-2000* (New York: Penguin Books); Niall Ferguson, 2004, *Colossus: The Price of America's Empire* (New York: Penguin).

17   Rogers M. Smith, 1997, *Civic Ideals: Conflicting Visions of Citizenship in U.S. History* (New Haven, CT: Yale University Press).

18   Of course, the economic motivation for transnational immigration can in particular circumstances "unmix" national heterogeneity. Rogers Brubaker, 1995, "Aftermaths of Empire and the Unmixing of People: Historical and Comparative Perspectives," *Ethnic & Racial Studies* 18:189–218.

19   Louis Althusser, 2001, "Ideology and Ideological State Apparatus (Notes Towards an Investigation)," pp. 85–126 in *Lenin and Philosophy, and Other Essays* (New York: Monthly Review Press).

20 Max Weber, 1978, *Economy and Society: An Outline of Interpretive Sociology* (Berkeley: University of California Press): 946 (my emphasis).

CONCLUSION

1 For example, see John C. Eastman, 2006, "From Feudalism to Consent: Rethinking Birthright Citizenship," *Legal Memorandum* 18:1–8; and John C. Eastman, 2008, "Born in the USA? Rethinking Birthright Citizenship in the Wake of 9/11," *University of Richmond Law Review* 42:955–968.

2 Ibid. 960.

3 Pierre Bourdieu and Loïc J. D. Wacquant, 1992, *An Invitation to Reflexive Sociology* (Chicago: University of Chicago Press).

BIBLIOGRAPHY

PRIMARY SOURCES

U.S. Congress Legislative Debates

Reconstruction Bill / Wade-Davis Bill (HR 244). 1864. *Congressional Globe*, 38th Congress, Session I, pp. 1249–1250, 2117, 2510, 3406, 3457–3461, 3482, 3491, 3544, 3448–3454.

An Act to amend several Acts heretofore passed to provide for the Enrolling and Calling out the National Forces, and for other Purposes, section 21 (HR 678). 1865. *Congressional Globe*, 38th Congress, Session II, pp. 280, 298, 338, 631–643, 974–980, 1034–1036, 1074–1085, 1114–1123, 1154–1161, 1169, 1237.

An Act for the Relief of certain Soldiers and Sailors therein designated (HR 108). 1867. *Congressional Globe*, 40th Congress, Session I, pp. 480, 564–565, 586, 591–592, 606, 644–649, 660–664, 677–678, 690–691, 695, 697–698, 740.

An Act concerning Rights of American Citizens in foreign States / 1868 Expatriation Act (HR 768). 1868. *Congressional Globe*, 40th Congress, Session II, pp. 1294, 1797–1806, 2030, 2217, 2311–2318, 2329, 3382, 3504, 3818, 3901–3902, 3986, 4096–4097, 4123, 4148, 4204, 4211, 4231–4238, 4236, 4328–4333, 4349–4360, 4445–4446, 4451, 4454, 4474, 4485, 4498.

An Act in Reference to the expatriation of citizens and their protection abroad / 1907 Expatriation Act (HR 24122). 1907. *Congressional Record*, 59th Congress, Session II, pp. 1120, 1377, 1463, 1467, 1501, 4197, 4263–4264, 4378, 4405, 4498–4499, 4630.

An Act amending section 1998 of the Revised Statutes of the United States, and to authorize the President, in certain cases, to mitigate or remit the loss of rights of citizenship imposed by law upon deserters from the naval service (HR 17483). 1912. *Congressional Record*, 62nd Congress, Session II, pp. 2903–2905, 2957, 8988, 9542, 11131, 11168, 11228, 11327, 11744.

An Act to revise and codify the nationality laws of the United States into a comprehensive nationality code / Nationality Act of 1940 (HR 9980). 1940. *Congressional Record*, 76th Congress, Session III, pp. 7633, 11939–11965, 11990, 12430–12431, 12816–12818, 12997, 13244–13250, 13183–13184, 13290, 13348, 13412–13413, 13591.

An Act to provide for loss of United States nationality under certain circumstances (HR 4103). 1944. *Congressional Record*, 78th Congress, Session II, pp. 1778–1789, 1981–1992, 2054, 6459, 6617.

An Act to revise the laws relating to immigration, naturalization, and nationality; and for other purposes / 1952 Walter Immigration Bill (HR 5678). 1952. *Congressional*

Record, 82nd Congress, Session II, pp. 1053, 2140, 2227, 4301–4321, 4399–4416, 4422–4444, 4450, 4665, 5803–5804, 5862–5863, 6947–6951, 6972–6991, 7016–7019, 7167, 8082–8085, 8214–8226, 8253–8268.

An Act to Amend the Immigration and Nationality Act to provide for the loss of nationality of persons convicted of certain crimes / Expatriation Act of 1954 (HR 7130). 1954. *Congressional Record*, 83rd Congress, Session II, pp. 10975, 11279–11283, 11359, 13002–13003, 14054, 14930, 14981, 14983, 15235–15236, 15559–15560, 15836–15837.

Terrorist Expatriation Act (S. 3327). 2010. *Congressional Record*, 111th Congress, Session II, pp. 1–3.

U.S. Public Laws

1906: Public Law No. 338, 34 *Stat.* 596–607.
1907: Public Law No, 193, 34 *Stat.* 1228–1229.
1912: Public Law No. 291, 37 *Stat.* 357.
1917: Public Law 65–12, 40 *Stat.* 76.
1934: Public Law No. 250, 48 *Stat.* 797–798.
1940: Public Law 76–876, 54 *Stat.* 1137–1174.
1944: Public Law 405–78, 58 *Stat.* 677.
1952: Public Law 82–414, 66 *Stat.* 267–272.
1954: Public Law 772–83, 68 *Stat.* 1146.
1961: Public Law 87–301, 75 *Stat.* 656.
1976: Public Law 94–412, 90 *Stat.* 1259.
1978: Public Law 95–432, 92 *Stat.* 1046.
1981: Public Law 97–116, 95 *Stat.* 1620–1621.
1986: Public Law 99–653, 100 *Stat.* 3655, 3658.
1988: Public Law 100–525, 102 *Stat.* 2617–2618.
1994: Public Law 103–416, 108 *Stat.* 4305.

U.S. Code

1935: Title 8, Aliens and Citizenship, pp. 174–175.
1940: Title 8, Aliens and Citizenship, pp. 472–472–473, 478, 481.
1958: Title 8, Aliens and Citizenship, pp. 849–850, 926–927, 934–935, 939–943; Title 18, Crimes and Criminal Procedure, pp. 3342–3347.
1994: Title 8, Aliens and Citizenship, pp. 286–289.
2000: Title 8, Aliens and Citizenship, pp. 1166–1170.
2004: Title 8, Aliens and Citizenship, pp. 832–833.

U.S. Court Cases

Talbot v. Janson, 3, 164 (1795).
United States v. Wong Kim Ark, 169 U.S. 649 (1898).
Brown v. Board of Education, 347 U.S. 483 (1954).
Trop v. Dulles, 356 U.S. 86 (1958).

Perez v. Brownell, 356 U.S. 44 (1958).

Baker v. Carr, 369 U.S, 186 (1962).

Schneider v. Rusk, 377 U.S, 163 (1964).

Griswold v. Connecticut, 381 U.S. 479 (1965).

Miranda v. Arizona, 384 U.S. 436 (1966).

Afroyim v. Rusk, 387 U.S. 255 (1967).

Rogers v. Bellei, 401 U.S. 819 (1971).

King v. Rogers, 463 F.2d 1188 (1972).

Davis v. District Director, Immigration and Naturalization Service, 481 F. Supp, 1178 (1979).

Vance v. Terrazas, 444 U.S. 252 (1980).

United States v. Schiffer, 831 F. Supp, 1166 (1993).

United States v. Kumpf, 438 U.S. 785 (2006).

U.S. Consular and Diplomatic Correspondence

Correspondence regarding American citizens in Turkey. 1871–1872. *Foreign Relations of the United States*, pp. 887–888.

Correspondence regarding American citizens in Turkey.1886–1887. *Foreign Relations of the United States*, pp. 862–864.

Correspondence regarding American citizens in Turkey. 1887–1888. *Foreign Relations of the United States*, pp. 1120–1125.

Correspondence regarding American citizens in Switzerland. 1887–1888. *Foreign Relations of the United States*, pp. 1073–1074.

Correspondence regarding American citizens in Germany. 1896. *Foreign Relations of the United States*, pp. 182–183.

Circulars, Passports for Persons Residing or Sojourning Abroad. 1899. *Foreign Relations of the United States*, pp. 1–4.

Circulars, Passports—Intent to return to the United States. 1902. *Foreign Relations of the United States*, p. 1.

Correspondence regarding American citizens in Switzerland. 1902. *Foreign Relations of the United States*, pp. 975–976.

Correspondence regarding American citizens in the Netherlands. 1906. *Foreign Relations of the United States*, part 1, pp. 4–5.

Expatriation. 1907. *Foreign Relations of the United States*, part 1, pp. 3–5.

Registration of Women who desire to resume or retain American citizenship. 1907. *Foreign Relations of the United States*, part 1, pp. 10–13.

Correspondence regarding American citizens in Portugal. 1907. *Foreign Relations of the United States*, part 2, pp. 958.

Expatriation and protection of Americans in China. 1908. *Foreign Relations of the United States*, pp. 1–2.

Expatriation. 1910. *Foreign Relations of the United States*, pp. 1–3.

Expatriation. 1911. *Foreign Relations of the United States*, pp. 1–2.

Expatriation of naturalized citizens. 1913. *Foreign Relations of the United States*, p. 3.

Conditions of Enlistment of Americans in foreign armies involving their expatriations. 1915. *Foreign Relations of the United States*, p. 25.

Proposed return to the United States of Naturalized citizens against whom the presumption of expatriation has arisen. 1916. *Foreign Relations of the United States*, pp. 10–11.

Correspondence regarding military service conventions. 1918. *Foreign Relations of the United States*, World War Supplement 2, pp. 648–732.

Proposals to European countries for agreements and treaties regarding naturalization, dual nationality, and military service. 1928. *Foreign Relations of the United States*, vol. 1, pp. 494–505.

Communication of negotiations with certain European Countries for agreements and treaties regarding naturalization, dual nationality, and military service. 1929. *Foreign Relations of the United States*, vol. 1, pp. 439–486.

U.S. International Treaties

Convention—Württemberg (1868), 18 *Stat.* 811–812.

Treaty with the King of Prussia (1868), 15 *Stat.* 615–617.

Treaty with Bavaria (1868), 15 *Stat.* 661–666.

Convention with Mexico (1868), 15 *Stat.* 679–685.

Treaty with the Grand Duchy of Baden (1868), 16 *Stat.* 731–734.

Convention with the Grand Duchy of Hesse (1868), 16 *Stat.* 743–746.

Convention with Belgium (1868), 16 *Stat.* 747–749.

Convention with Sweden and Norway (1869), 17 *Stat.* 809–813.

Convention—Austro-Hungarian Monarchy (1870), 17 *Stat.* 833–837.

Convention with Great Britain (1871), 17 *Stat.* 841–843.

Convention—Denmark (1872), 17 *Stat.* 941–944.

Treaty—Haiti (1902), 33 *Stat.* 2101–2104.

Convention—Repatriation—Inter-American Convention (1906), 37 *Stat.* 1653–1657.

Naturalization Convention—Peru (1907), 36 *Stat.* 2181–2183.

Naturalization Convention—Portugal (1908), 35 *Stat.* 1902–1909.

Naturalization Convention—Salvador (1908), 35 *Stat.* 2038–2040.

Naturalization Convention—Honduras (1908), 36 *Stat.* 2160–2162.

Naturalization Convention—Uruguay (1908), 36 *Stat.* 2165–2168.

Naturalization Convention—Brazil (1908), 36 *Stat.* 2444–2447.

Naturalization Convention—Nicaragua (1908), 37 *Stat.* 1560–1564.

Naturalization Convention—Costa Rica (1911), 37 *Stat.* 1063–1760.

Military Service—Great Britain (1918), 12 *Bevans* 379–384.

Military Service—Canada (1918), 12 *Bevans* 385–387.

Military Service—Italy (1918), 9 *Bevans* 136–138.

Military Service—Greece (1918), 8 *Bevans* 320–322.

Military Service—France (1918), 7 *Bevans* 896–898.

Naturalization Treaty—Bulgaria (1923), 5 Bevans, pp. 1083–1085.

Naturalization Convention—Czechoslovakia (1928), 46 *Stat.* 2424–2426.

League of Nations. April 13, 1930. *Convention on Certain Questions Relating to the Conflict of Nationality Law*. League of Nations, Treaty Series, vol. 179, p. 89, no. 4137.

Military Obligations in Certain Cases of Double Nationality (1930), 2 *Bevans* 1049–1054.

Military Service: Dual Nationality—Norway (1930), 10 *Bevans* 503–504.

Naturalization Treaty—Albania (1932), 49 *Stat*. 3241–3244.

Military Service: Dual Nationality—Sweden (1933), 11 *Bevans* 778–779.

Pan-American Convention on the Nationality of Women (1933), 49 *Stat*. 2957–2966.

Lithuania—Military Service (1937), 53 *Stat*. 1569–1572.

Military Service and Dual Nationality—Switzerland (1937), 11 *Bevans* 936–937.

Military Obligations of Persons Having Dual Nationality—Finland (1939), 7 *Bevans* 747–748.

Military Service—Australia (1942), 5 *Bevans* 150–154.

Military Service—Belgium (1942), 5 *Bevans* 575–581.

Military Service—Canada (1942), 6 *Bevans* 268–273.

Military Service—Norway (1942), 10 *Bevans* 540–544.

Military Service—Poland (1942), 11 *Bevans* 277–282.

Military Service—Yugoslavia (1942), 12 *Bevans* 1267–1270.

Military Service—Brazil (1943), 5 *Bevans* 955–959.

Military Service—Cuba (1943), 6 *Bevans* 1216–1220.

Military Service—Czecholovakia (1943), 6 *Bevans* 1304–1308.

Military Service—Ecuador (1945), 7 *Bevans* 405–407.

Military Obligations of Persons Having Dual Nationality—France (1948), 7 *Bevans* 1242–1244, 1294–1295.

U.N. General Assembly. August 30, 1961. *Convention on the Reduction of Statelessness*. United Nations, Treaty Series, vol. 989, p. 175.

Council of Europe. 1963. *Convention on the Reduction of Cases of Multiple Nationality and Military Obligations in Cases of Multiple Nationality*. European Treaty Series 43.

Council of Europe. 1977. *Protocol Amending the Convention on the Reduction of Cases of Multiple Nationality and Military Obligations in Cases of Multiple Nationality*. European Treaty Series 95.

Council of Europe. 1977. *Additional Protocol Amending the Convention on the Reduction of Cases of Multiple Nationality and Military Obligations in Cases of Multiple Nationality*. European Treaty Series 96.

Council of Europe. 1993. *Second Protocol Amending the Convention on the Reduction of Cases of Multiple Nationality and Military Obligations in Cases of Multiple Nationality*. European Treaty Series 95.

Council of Europe. 1997. *European Convention on Nationality*, European Treaty Series 166.

U.S. State Department Documents

Department of State, *Decisions of the Board of Appellate Review*. Vol. 5 (1980–1982).

Department of State, *Decisions of the Board of Appellate Review*. Vol. 6 (1982).

Department of State, *Decisions of the Board of Appellate Review.* Vol. 7 (1983).
Department of State, *Decisions of the Board of Appellate Review.* Vols. 8–9 (1984).
Department of State, *Decisions of the Board of Appellate Review.* Vols. 10–11 (1985).
Department of State, *Decisions of the Board of Appellate Review.* Vols. 12–13 (1986).
Department of State, *Opinions of the Board of Appellate Review.* Vols. 14–15 (1987).
Department of State, *Opinions of the Board of Appellate Review.* Vols. 16–17 (1988).
Department of State, *Opinions of the Board of Appellate Review.* Vols. 18–19 (1989).
Department of State, *Opinions of the Board of Appellate Review.* Vols. 20–21 (1990).
Department of State, *Opinions of the Board of Appellate Review.* Vol. 22 (1991–1993).
Department of State, *Published Opinions of the Board of Appellate Review.* Vol. 9 (1994–1996).

Canadian Documents

Canadian Citizenship Act of 1946. *Statutes of Canada* 1946, ch, 15.
Citizenship Act of 1977. *Statutes of Canada* 1974-75-76, ch, 108.
Bill C-63, *An Act respecting Canadian citizenship.* 1st Sess., 36th Parl. 1998 (not passed).
Bill C-16, *An Act respecting Canadian citizenship.* 2nd Sess., 36th Parl. 1999 (not passed).
Bill C-18, *An Act respecting Canadian citizenship.* 2nd Sess., 37th Parl. 2002 (not passed).
The Standing Senate Committee on Foreign Affairs and International Trade. 2007. *The Evacuation of Canadians from Lebanon in July 2006: Implication for the Government of Canada.* Ottawa, Canada.

Others

United States. 1810. "Resolution Proposing an Amendment to the Constitution of the United States." *Statutes at Large,* vol. 2, 11th Congress, Session II, p. 613.
Handwritten copy of Wade-Davis Bill as originally submitted. 1846. Records of Legislative Proceedings; Records of the United States House of Representatives, 1789–1946; Record Group 233. National Archives.
Grant, Ulysses S. December 1, 1873. *State of the Union* (Message of the President of the United States, with the accompanying documents, transmitted to the two Houses of Congress at the beginning of the first session of the Forty-third Congress). 43rd Congress, 1st Session, H. Exec. Doc. 1, pt. 1, v.1, Washington, DC: Government Printing Office.
House of Representatives. 1928. *Hearing before the committee on Foreign Affairs on HJR 195 and HJR 268.* 17th Congress, Session I, Serial No. 95. Washington, DC: Government Printing Office.
Eisenhower, Dwight D. January 7, 1954. *State of the Union* (Annual Message to the Congress on the State of the Union). Pp. 6–23 in *Public Papers of the Presidents of the United States 1954.* Washington, DC: Government Printing Office.
House of Representatives. 1986. *Hearing before the subcommittee on immigration, refugees, and international law of the Committee on the Judiciary on HR 4823, HR 4444*

and HR 2184. 99th Congress, Session II. Washington, DC: Government Printing Office.

Draft of *Domestic Security Enhancement Act of 2003*. January 9, 2003.Section-by-section analysis. Available at http://www.pbs.org/now/politics/patriot2-hi.pdf.

Yaser Esam Hamdi v. Donald Rumsfeld, Settlement Agreement, September 17, 2004. Available at http://news.findlaw.com/hdocs/docs/hamdi/91704stlagrmnt.html.

SECONDARY SOURCES

Abramson, Lawrence. 1984. "United States Loss of Citizenship Law after Terrazas: Decisions of the Board of Appellate Review." *New York University Journal of International Law and Politics* 16:829–880.

Agamben, Giorgio. 1998. *Homo Sacer: Sovereign Power and Bare Life*. Stanford, CA: Stanford University Press.

Aleinikoff, Alexander T. 1986. "Theories of Loss of Citizenship." *Michigan Law Review* 84:1471–1503.

———. 1998. *Between Principles and Politics: The Direction of U.S. Citizenship Policy*. Washington, DC: Carnegie Endowment for International Peace.

Aleinikoff, Alexander T., David A. Martin, and Hiroshi Motomura. 2003. *Immigration and Citizenship: Process and Policy*. St. Paul, MN: Thomson/West.

Alford, Robert R., and Roger Friedland. 1985. *Powers of Theory: Capitalism, the State, and Democracy*. Cambridge, UK: Cambridge University Press.

Althusser, Louis. 2001. "Ideology and Ideological State Apparatus (Notes Towards an Investigation)." Pp. 85–126 in *Lenin and Philosophy, and Other Essays*. New York: Monthly Review Press.

Anderson, Benedict. 1991. *Imagined Communities*. London: Verso.

Anderson, Fred, and Andrew Cayton. 2005. *The Dominion of War: Empire and Liberty in North America, 1500–2000*. New York: Penguin Books.

Appleman, Irving. 1968. "The Supreme Court on Expatriation: An Historical Review." *Federal Bar Journal* 23:351.

Arendt, Hannah. 1979. *The Origins of Totalitarianism*. New York: Harcourt.

———. 1994. *Eichmann in Jerusalem: A Report on the Banality of Evil*. New York: Penguin.

Bach, Stanley. 1990. "Suspension of the Rules, the Order of Business, and the Development of Congressional Procedure." *Legislative Studies Quarterly* 15:49–63.

Bauman, Zygmunt. 2004. *Wasted Lives: Modernity and Its Outcasts*. Oxford, UK: Polity.

Benhabib, Seyla. 2004. *The Rights of Others: Aliens, Residents and Citizens*. Cambridge, UK: Cambridge University Press.

Bevans, Charles I. 1976. *Treaties and Other International Agreements of the United States of America, 1776–1949*. Washington, DC: Department of States Publication.

Blatter, Joachim K., Sterfeanie Erdmann, and Katja Schwanke. 2009. *Acceptance of Dual Citizenship: Empirical Data and Political Contexts*. Lucerne: Institute of Political Science, University of Lucerne.

Bloemraad, Irene. 2007. "Much Ado about Nothing? The Contours of Dual Citizenship in the United States and Canada." Pp. 159–186 in *Dual Citizenship in Global Perspective: From Unitary to Multiple Citizenship*, edited by T. Faist, and P. Kivisto. New York: Palgrave Macmillan.

Boll, Alfred M. 2007. *Multiple Nationality and International Law*. Leiden, NDL: Martinus Nijhoff.

Borchard, Edwin Montefiore. 1928. *The Diplomatic Protection of Citizens Abroad; or, The Law of International Claims*. New York: Banks Law.

Boudin, Leonard B. 1960. "Involuntary Loss of American Nationality." *Harvard Law Review* 73:1510–1531.

Bourdieu, Pierre, and John B. Thompson. 1991. *Language and Symbolic Power*. Cambridge, MA: Harvard University Press.

———, and Loïc J. D. Wacquant. 1992. *An Invitation to Reflexive Sociology*. Chicago: University of Chicago Press.

Bredbenner, Candice Lewis. 1998. *A Nationality of Her Own: Women, Marriage, and the Law of Citizenship*. Berkeley: University of California Press.

Brubaker, Rogers. 1989a. "The French Revolution and the Invention of Citizenship." *French Politics and the Invention of Citizenship* 7:30–49.

———. 1989b. "Introduction." Pp. 1–27 in *Immigration and the Politics of Citizenship in Europe and North America*, edited by R. Brubaker. Lanham, MD: The German Marshall Fund of the United States, University Press of America.

———. 1992. *Citizenship and Nationhood in France and Germany*. Cambridge, UK: Harvard University Press.

———. 1995. "Aftermaths of Empire and the Unmixing of People: Historical and Comparative Perspectives." *Ethnic & Racial Studies* 18:189–218.

———. 1996. *Nationalism Reframed: Nationhood and the National Question in the New Europe*. New York: Cambridge University Press.

Campi, Alicia J. 2004. *The McCarran-Walter Act: A Contradictory Legacy on Race, Quotas, and Ideology*. Washington, DC: American Immigration Law Foundation.

Cashman, Edward J. 1967. "Fourteenth Amendment Precludes Involuntary Expatriation." *American University Law Review* 17:86.

Casper, Gerhard. 2008. "Forswearing Allegiance." *The Maurice and Muriel Fulton Lecture in Legal History*. Chicago: University of Chicago Law School.

Casper, Gerhard, and Stephen D. Krasner. 2009. "On Citizenship." Review of Peter J. Spiro, *Beyond Citizenship: American Identity After Globalization. American Interest* 4:111–116.

Checkel, Jeffrey T. 2001. "The Europeanization of Citizenship?" Pp. 180–197 in *Transforming Europe: Europeanization and Domestic Change*, edited by M. G. Cowles, J. Caporaso, and T. Risse. Ithaca, NY: Cornell University Press.

Chopin, Isabelle. 2006. "Administrative Practices in the Acquistion of Nationality." Pp. 221–268 in *Acquisition and Loss of Nationality: Policies and Trends in 15 European Countires*, Vol. 1: *Comparative Analyses*, edited by R. Baubock, E. Ersboll, K. Groenendijk, and H. Waldrauch. Amsterdam: Amsterdam University Press.

Cohen, Elizabeth F. 2009. *Semi-Citizenship in Democratic Politics*. New York: Cambridge University Press.

———. 2011. "Reconsidering U.S. Immigration Reform: The Temporal Principle of Citizenship." *Perspectives on Politics* 9:575–583.

Cohen, Elliot. 1985. *Citizens and Soldiers: The Dilemmas of Military Service*. Ithaca, NY: Cornell University Press.

Collins, Donald E. 1985. *Native American Aliens: Disloyalty and the Renunciation of Citizenship by Japanese Americans during World War II*. Westport, CT: Greenwood.

Conover, Pamela Johnston, Ivor M. Crewe, and Donald D. Searing. 1991. "The Nature of Citizenship in the United States and Great Britain: Empirical Comments on Theoretical Themes." *Journal of Politics* 53:800–832.

Cott, Nancy F. 1998. "Marriage and Women's Citizenship in the United States, 1830–1934." *American Historical Review* 103:1440–1474.

Cowen, Deborah, and Emily Gilbert. 2008. "War, Citizenship, Territory." New York: Routledge.

Cruikshank, Barbara. 1999. *The Will to Empower: Democratic Citizens and Other Subjects*. Ithaca, NY: Cornell University Press.

Dagger, Richard. 1997. *Civic Virtues: Rights, Citizenship, and Republican Liberalism*. New York: Oxford University Press.

Daley, James. 1958. "Loss of Nationality by Service in a Foreign Army." *Wyoming Law Journal* 14:258.

Dienstag, Abbe L. 1982. "*Fedorenko v. United States*: War Crimes, the Defense of Duress, and American Nationality Law." *Columbia Law Review* 82:120–183.

Donner, Ruth. 1994. *The Regulation of Nationality in International Law*. Irvington-on-Hudson, NY: Transnational Publishers.

Dugard, John. 1980. "South Africa's 'Independent' Homelands: An Exercise in Denationalization." *Denver Journal of International Law and Policy* 10:11–36.

Eastman, John C. 2006. "From Feudalism to Consent: Rethinking Birthright Citizenship." *Legal Memorandum* 18:1–8.

———. 2006. "Born in the USA? Rethinking Birthright Citizenship in the Wake of 9/11." *University of Richmond Law Review* 42: 955–968.

Eliot, Charles William. 1897. *American Contribution to Civilization and Other Essays and Addresses*. New York: The Century Co.

Ellis, Lewis Ethan. 1961. *Frank B. Kellogg and American Foreign Relations, 1925–1929*. New Brunswick, NJ: Rutgers University Press.

Ferguson, Niall. 2004. *Colossus: The Price of America's Empire*. New York: Penguin.

Flournoy, Richard W. Jr. 1930. "Nationality Convention, Protocols and Recommendations Adopted by the First Conference on the Codification of International Law." *The American Journal of International Law* 24:467–485.

Gellner, Ernest. 1983. *Nations and Nationalism*. Ithaca, NY: Cornell University Press.

Glass, Joseph B. 2002. *From New Zion to Old Zion: American Jewish Immigration and Settlement in Palestine, 1917–1939*. Detroit, MI: Wayne State University Press.

Glazer, Nathan. 2002. "Dual Citizenship as a Challenge to Sovereignty." Pp. 33–54 in *Sovereignty Under Challenge: How Governments Respond*, edited by J. D. Montgomeryand N. Glazer. New Brunswick, NJ: Transaction.

Goldberg, Chad Alan. 2007. *Citizens and Paupers: Relief, Rights and Race from the Freedmen's Bureau to Workfare*. Chicago: University of Chicago Press.

Goodman, Steven S. 1988. "Protecting Citizenship: Strengthening the Intent Requirement in Expatriation Proceedings." *George Washington Law Review* 56.

Graham, Nora. 2004. "Patriot Act II and Denationalization: An Unconstitutional Attempt to Revive Stripping Americans of Their Citizenship." *Cleveland State Law Review* 52:593.

Green, Nancy L., and Francois Weil. 2007. *Citizenship and Those Who Leave: The Politics of Emigration and Expatriation*. Urbana: University of Illinois Press.

Griffith, Elwin. 1988. "Expatriation and the American Citizen." *Howard Law Review* 31:494.

Gross, Emanuel. 2003. "Defensive Democracy: Is It Possible to Revoke the Citizenship, Deport, or Negate the Civil Rights of a Person Instigating Terrorist Action against His Own State?" *University of Missouri–Kansas City Law Review* 72:51.

Grotelueschen, Mark E. 2007. *The AEF Way of War: The American Army and Combat in World War I*. Cambridge, UK: Cambridge University Press.

Hammar, Tomas. 1985. "Dual Citizenship and Political Integration." *International Migration Review* 19:438–450.

Hart, Gideon M. 2010. "The 'Original' Thirteenth Amendment: The Misunderstood Titles of Nobility Amendment." *Marquette Law Review* 94:311–371.

Herzog, Ben. 2009. "Between Nationalism and Humanitarianism: The Global Discourse on Refugees." *Nations and Nationalism* 15:185–205.

Hobbes, Thomas. [1651] 1996. *Leviathan,*. edited by R. Tuck. Cambridge, UK: Cambridge University Press.

Horwitz, Morton J. 1998. *The Warren Court and the Pursuit of Justice: A Critical Issue*. New York: Hill and Wang.

Howard, Marc Moje. 2005. "Variation in Dual Citizenship in the Countries of the E.U." *International Migration Review* 39:697–720.

Hudson, Manley O. 1930. "The First Conference for the Codification of International Law." *American Journal of International Law* 24:447–466.

Irving, Helen. 2004. "Citizenship and Subject-Hood in Twentieth-Century Australia." Pp. 9–18 in *From Subjects to Citizens: A Hundred Years of Citizenship in Australia and Canada*, edited by P. Boyer, L. Cardinal, and D. Headon. Ottawa: University of Ottawa Press.

Isin, Engin F., and Patricia K. Wood. 1999. *Citizenship and Identity*. Thousand Oaks, CA: Sage.

Jacobson, David. 1996. *Rights across Borders: Immigration and the Decline of Citizenship*. Baltimore, MD: Johns Hopkins University Press.

James, Alan G. 1986. "The Board of Appellate Review of the Department of State: The Right to Appellate Review of Administrative Determinations of Loss of Nationality." *San Diego Law Review* 23:261–326.

———. 1990. "Expatriation in the United States: Precepts and Practice Today and Yesterday." *San Diego Law Review* 27:853–905.

———. 1991. "Cult-Induced Renunciation of United States Citizenship: The Involuntary Expatriation of Black Hebrews." *San Diego Law Review* 25:645–670.

Janoski, Thomas. 1998. *Citizenship and Civil Society: A Framework of Rights and Obligations in Liberal, Traditional, and Social Democratic Regimes.* Cambridge, UK: Cambridge University Press.

Jones-Cerrera, Michael. 2001. "Under Two Flags: Dual Nationality in Latin America and Its Consequences for Naturalization in the United States." *International Migration Review* 35:997–1029.

Joppke, Christian, and Zeev Roshenhek. 2001. "Ethnic-Priority Immigration in Israel and Germany: Resilience Versus Demise." The Center for Comparative Immigration Studies, University of California San Diego.

Kelly, Henry Ansgar. 1991. "Dual Nationality, the Myth of Election, and a Kinder, Gentler State Department." *University of Miami Inter-American Law Review* 23:421–464.

Kemp, Adriana. 1999. "The Mirror Language of the Border: Territorial Borders and the Constitution of a National Minority in Israel." *Sociologia Israelit* 3:319–350.

Kennedy, Charles Stuart. 1994. "Interview with Alan G. James." The Foreign Affairs Oral History Collection of the Association for Diplomatic Studies and Training, Washington, DC.

Kerber, Linda K. 2007. "Presidential Address: The Stateless as the Citizen's Other: A View from the United States." *American Historical Review* 112:1–34.

Kettner, James H. 1974. "The Deveopement of American Citizenship in the Revolutionary Era: The Idea of Volitional Allegiance." *American Journal of Legal History* 18:208–242.

Kingston, Rebecca. 2005. "The Unmaking of Citizens: Banishment and the Modern Citizenship Regime in France." *Citizenship Studies* 9:23–40.

Kivisto, Peter, and Thomas Faist. 2007. *Citizenship: Discourse, Theory, and Transnational Prospects.* Malden, MA: Blackwell.

Koslowski, Rey. 2002. "Challenges of International Cooperation in a World of Increasing Dual Citizenship." Pp. 157–182 in *Rights and Duties of Dual Nationals: Evolution and Prospects*, edited by D. Martin and K. Hailbronner. Leiden, NDL: Brill Academic Publishers.

Kymlicka, Will. 1995. *Multicultural Citizenship: A Liberal Theory of Minority Rights.* Oxford, UK: Clarendon.

Lavi, Shai. 2011. "Citizenship Revocation as Punishment: On the Modern Duties of Citizens and Their Criminal Breach." *University of Toronto Law Journal* 61:783–810.

Lewis, Charles, and Adam Mayle. 2003. "Justice Department Drafts Sweeping Expansion of Anti-Terrorism Act." The Center for Public Integrity. Available at http://www.publicintegrity.org/2003/02/07/3159/justice-dept-drafts-sweeping-expansion-anti-terrorism-act.

Mann, Michael. 1987. "Ruling Class Strategies and Citizenship." *Sociology* 21:339–354.

———. 1988. *States, War and Capitalism: Studies in Political Sociology*. Oxford, UK: Basil Blackwell.

———. 1993. "Nation-States in Europe and Other Continents: Diversifying, Developing, Not Dying." *Daedalus* 122:115–140.

Manza, Jeff, and Christopher Uggen. 2006. *Locked Out: Felon Disenfranchisement and American Democracy*, edited by M. Tonry, and N. Morris. Oxford, UK: Oxford University Press.

Mariner, Joanne. 2004. "Patriot II's Attack on Citizenship." June 22. *CNN.com*.

Martin, David. 1999. "New Rules on Dual Nationality for a Democratizing Globe: Between Rejection and Embrace." *Georgetown Immigration Law Journal* 14:1–34.

———. 2004. "Dual Nationality: TR's 'Self-Evident Absurdity.'*Chair Lecture*. University of Virginia School of Law.

Mathisen, Ralph W. 2006. "Peregrini, Barbari, and Cives Romani: Concepts of Citizenship and the Legal Identity of Barbarians in the Later Roman Empire." *American Historical Review* 11:1011–1040.

Matteo, Henry S. 1997. *Denationalization v. "The Right to Have Rights": The Standard of Intent in Citizenship Loss*. Lanham, MD: University Press of America.

Menton, Linda K. 1994. "Research Report: Nisei Soldiers at Dachau, Spring 1945." *Holocaust and Genocide Studies* 8:258–274.

Miller, David. 2000. *Citizenship and National Identity*. Cambridge, UK: Polity.

Miller, Hunter. 1930. "The Hague Codification Conference." *American Journal of International Law* 24:674–693.

Minahan, James. 2002. *Encyclopedia of the Stateless Nations: Ethnic and Natoinal Groups around the World*. London: Greenwood.

Moore, John Bassett. 1906. *A Digest of International Law*, vol. 3. Washington, DC: Government Printing Office.

Neuman, Gerald L. 1994. "Justifying U.S. Naturalization Policies." *Immigration and Nationality Law Revew* 16:83–126.

Nicolosi, Ann Marie. 2001. "'We Do Not Want Our Girls to Mary Foreigners': Gender, Race, and American Citizenship." *National Women's Studies Association Journal* 13:1–21.

Noiriel, Gérard. 1996. *The French Melting Pot: Immigration, Citizenship, and National Identity*, vol. 5. Minneapolis: University of Minnesota Press.

Nyers, Peter. 2009. *Securitization of Citizenship*. New York: Routledge.

———. 2010. "Dueling Designs: The Politics of Rescuing Dual Citizens." *Citizenship Studies* 14:47–60.

Ong, Aihwa. 1999. *Flexible Citizenship: The Cultural Logic of Transnationality*. Durham: Duke University Press.

Pateman, Carole. 1998. *The Sexual Contract*. Cambridge, UK: Polity.

Peled, Yoav. 1992. "Ethnic Democracy and the Legal Construction of Citizenship: Arab Citizens of the Jewish State." *American Political Science Review* 86:432.

Pickering, Margaret S., Sally J. Cummins, and David P. Stewart. 2002. "Digest of United States Practice in International Law, 1989–1990." Washington, DC: International Law Institute.

Renshon, Stanley A. 2005. *The 50% American: Immigration and National Identity in an Age of Terror*. Washington, DC: Georgetown University Press.

Román, Ediberto. 2006. "The Citizenship Dialectic." *Georgetown Immigration Law Journal* 20: 557–610.

———. 2013. *Those Damned Immigrants: America's Hysteria over Undocumented Immigration*. New York: New York University Press.

Ronner, Amy D. 2005. "Denaturalization and Death: What It Means to Preclude the Exercise of Judicial Discretion." *Georgetown Immigration Law Journal* 20:101–132.

Rousseau, Jean Jacques. [1762] 1997. "Of the Social Contract or Principles of Political Right." In *The Social Contract and Other Political Writings*, edited by V. Gourevitch. Cambridge, UK: Cambridge University Press.

Said, Edward W. 1978. *Orientalism*. New York: Vintage.

Scahill, Timothy. 2006. "The Domestic Security Enhancement Act of 2003: A Glimpse into a Post–Patriot Act Approach to Combating Domestic Terrorism." *CR: The New Centennial Review* 6: 69–94.

Scherner-Kim, Karen. 2000. "The Role of the Oath of Renunciation in Current U.S. Nationality Policy—To Enforce, To Omit, or Maybe To Change." *Georgetown Law Journal* 88: 329–380.

Schmitt, Carl. 1976. *The Concept of the Political*. New Brunswick, NJ: Rutgers University Press.

———. 1985. *Political Theology: Four Chapters on the Concept of Sovereignty*. Cambridge, MA: MIT Press.

Schuck, Peter H. 1998. *Citizens, Strangers, and In-Betweens: Essays on Immigration and Citizenship*. Boulder, CO: Westview.

———, and Rogers M. Smith. 1985. *Citizenship Without Consent: Illegal Aliens in the American Polity*. New Haven, CT: Yale University Press.

Schwartz, Bernard. 1996. *The Warren Court: A Retrospective*. Oxford, UK: Oxford University Press.

Schwartz, David F. 1982. "Citizenship after Afroyim and Bellei: Continuing Controversy." *Hasting Constitutional Law Quarterly* 2:1003.

Sejersen, Tanja B. 2008. "'I Vow to Thee My Country'—The Expansion of Dual Citizenship in the 21st Century." *International Migration Review* 42:523–549.

Shafir, Gershon, and Yoav Peled. 2002. *Being Israeli: The Dynamics of Multiple Citizenship*. Cambridge, UK: Cambridge University Press.

Shalins, Peter. 2004. *Unnaturally French: Foreign Citizens in the Old Regime and After*. Ithaca: Cornell University Press.

Shklar, Judith N. 1991. *American Citizenship: The Quest for Inclusion*. Cambridge, MA: Harvard University Press.

Silversmith, Jol A. 1999. "The Missing Thirteenth Amendment: Constitutional Nonsense and Titles of Nobility." *Southern California Interdisciplinary Law Journal* 8:577–612.

Smith, Rogers M. 1997. *Civic Ideals: Conflicting Visions of Citizenship in U.S. History.* New Haven, CT Yale University Press.

Spiro, Peter J. 1997. "Dual Nationality and the Meaning of Citizenship." *Emory Law Review* 46:1411–1486.

———. 1998. "Questioning Barriers to Naturalization." *Georgetown Immigration Law Journal* 13:479–519.

———. 2002a. "Embracing Dual Nationality." Pp. 19–33 in *Dual Nationality, Social Rights, and Federal Citizenship in the U.S. and Europe: The Reinvention of Citizenship*, edited by R. Hansen and P. Weil. New York: Berghahn.

———. 2002b. "Political Rights and Dual Nationality." Pp. 135–152 in *Rights and Duties of Dual Nationals: Evolution and Prospects*, edited by D. Martin and K. Hailbronner. Leiden, NLD: Brill.

———. 2008. *Beyond Citizenship: American Identity after Globalization*. Oxford, UK: Oxford University Press.

Staton, Jeffrey K., Robert Jackson, and Damarys Canache. 2007. "Costly Citizenship? Dual Nationality Institutions, Naturalization, and Political Connectedness." Social Science Research Network. Available at http://ssrn.com/abstract=995569.

Torpey, John C. 2000. *The Invention of the Passport: Surveillance, Citizenship, and the State*. Cambridge, UK: Cambridge University Press.

United States. 2001. *Citizenship Laws of the World*. Washington, DC: U.S. Office of Personnel Management, Investigations Service.

Van Dyne, Frederick. 1904. *Citizenship of the United State*. Rochester, NY: Lawyers' Co-operative.

Walter, Michael. 1978. "The Bancroft Conventions: Second-Class Citizenship for Naturalized Americans." *International Lawyer* 12:825–833.

Walzer, Michael. 1983. *Spheres of Justice: A Defense of Pluralism and Equality*. Oxford: Martin Robertson.

———. 1992. *What It Means to Be an American*. New York: Marsilio.

Weber, Max. 1978. *Economy and Society: An Outline of Interpretive Sociology*. Berkeley: University of California Press.

Weil, Patrick. 2001. "Access to Citizenship: A Comparison of Twenty-Five Nationality Laws." Pp. 17–35 in *Citizenship Today: Global Perspectives and Practices*, edited by T. A. Aleinikoff and D. Klusmeyer. Washington, DC: Brooklings Institution.

———. 2008. *How to be French: Nationality in the Making since 1789*. Durham, NC: Duke University Press.

———. 2013. *The Sovereign Citizen: Denationalization and the Origins of the American Republic*. Philadephia: University of Pennsylvania Press.

Weissbrodt, David, and Laura Danielson. 2005. *Immigration Law and Procedure in a Nutshell*. St. Paul, MN: Thomson/ West.

Wells, Charlotte C. 1995. *Law and Citizenship in Early Modern France*. Baltimore, MD: Johns Hopkins University Press.

Wharton, Francis. 1886. *A Digest of the International Law of the United States: Taken from Documents Issued by Presidents and Secretaries of State, and from Decisions of Federal Courts and Opinions of Attorneys-General*. Washington, DC: Government Printing Office.

Wright, Joanne H. 2002. "Going Against the Grain: Hobbes's Case for Original Maternal Dominion." *Journal of Women's History* 14:123–155.

INDEX

ABOUT THE AUTHOR

Ben Herzog is Lecturer (equivalent to Assistant Professor in the United States) at the Ben-Gurion Research Institute, at the Ben-Gurion University of the Negev. In 2012–2013, he served as the William Lyon Mackenzie King Research Fellow at the Canada Program of Harvard's Weatherhead Center for International Affairs. His primary teaching and research interests are Sociology of Law, Immigration, and Citizenship; Qualitative and Comparative Historical Methods; Political Sociology; and North American and Middle Eastern History and Politics. He has also served as the Pierre Keller Post-Doctoral Fellow in Transatlantic Relations with the Jackson Institute for Global Affairs at Yale University and as a Visiting Assistant Professor of Sociology at Dartmouth College. His articles on refugees and citizenship have been published in *Nations and Nationalism, Israel Studies Forum, Research in Political Sociology, European Journal of Sociology, Eastern European Politics and Society*, and *Citizenship Studies*.